The Hoo Peninsula Landscape

The Hoo Peninsula Landscape

Sarah Newsome, Edward Carpenter and Peter Kendall

Published by Historic England, The Engine House, Fire Fly Avenue, Swindon SN2 2EH
www.HistoricEngland.org.uk

Historic England is a Government service championing England's heritage and giving expert, constructive advice, and the English Heritage Trust is a charity caring for the National Heritage Collection of more than 400 historic properties and their collections.

Images (except as otherwise shown) © Historic England, © Crown Copyright. HE, or Reproduced by permission of Historic England
Shuttle Radar Topography Mission (SRTM) data (on Fig 2 and inside back cover) courtesy of the CGIAR Consortium for Spatial Information.

First published 2015

ISBN 978-1-84802-225-6

British Library Cataloguing in Publication data
A CIP catalogue record for this book is available from the British Library.

Application for the reproduction of images should be made to Historic England. Every effort has been made to trace the copyright holders and we apologise in advance for any unintentional omissions, which we would be pleased to correct in any subsequent edition of this book.

For more information about images from the Archive, contact Archives Services Team, Historic England, The Engine House, Fire Fly Avenue, Swindon SN2 2EH; telephone (01793) 414600.

Brought to publication by Sarah Enticknap, Publishing, Historic England.

Typeset in Georgia Pro Light 9.25/13pt

Edited by Jenny Lawson
Page layout by Hybert Design
Printed in the UK by Bell & Bain

Front Cover
View looking west across the Hoo Peninsula with the Grain industrial area in the foreground.
[26477/050]

Inside front cover
Control room at Kingsnorth Power Station.
[DP172037]

Frontispiece
Vessels moored in the Medway estuary off Port Victoria, Isle of Grain in 1951. The site of an old salt works is visible in the foreground.
[Aerofilms EAW038192]

Foreword
View looking east of cattle on Allhallows Marshes with the Grain industrial area visible in the background.
[DP172017]

Contents

Foreword

This informative, illuminating and very welcome book successfully explores thousands of years of the Hoo Peninsula's history, its people and the perceptions others have of it. The authors are to be congratulated, because whether your interests lie in lollardy*, medieval farming methods, military history, modern history or nature, you will find some nugget of information at the turn of a page. Charles Dickens spent part of his childhood on the Hoo Peninsula, and in Great Expectations describes the marshes and their people better than anyone: 'The dark flat wilderness, intersected with dykes and mounds and gates, with scattered cattle feeding on it was the marshes; ... the low leaden line beyond was the river; and ... the distant savage lair from which the wind was rushing, was the sea...'. I recognise Dickens's description, but my personal experience of the Hoo Peninsula is not just its romantic, desolate marshes and unique skies and landscapes, but most importantly the kindness and good nature of its inhabitants who, like me, I am sure, will be fascinated by this book.

*Lollardy was a religious and political movement of the 14–16th centuries. As a leading lollard, Sir John Oldcastle of Cooling Castle was convicted as a heretic and executed in 1417.

Jools Holland OBE DL

Acknowledgements

The authors would like to thank everyone who commented on the draft book text or contributed to the Hoo Peninsula Historic Landscape Project on which this book is based. The modern photographs, with the exception of those taken by the authors, are by Steve Cole, James O Davies, Damian Grady, Derek Kendall and Pat Payne. The illustrations were mainly produced by Phil Sinton alongside contributions by Peter Dunn, Sharon Soutar and Vince Griffin. We are grateful to Foster + Partners, Land Securities, Kent History and Library Centre, National Library of Scotland, John Minnis and Victor Smith for allowing us to reproduce their images in the book.

Our landscape is continually changing. The Hoo Peninsula, which extends into the Thames Estuary from the north Kent coast, has a unique and varied character that reflects how its landscape has been used over thousands of years (Fig 1). Two factors have strongly influenced the peninsula's development over time. First, its location on the River Thames, the country's most important shipping route, close to the markets and centres of power in London and neighbouring the important naval and garrison towns of Chatham and Sheerness, has made it a desirable setting for vital defence installations and industries (Fig 2). Second, physical features of the peninsula, such as its river estuaries and resources, have provided the environment needed to sustain these industries, develop new technologies and, from the medieval period onwards, undertake major land reclamation. This unique combination of factors has allowed the Hoo Peninsula to play an important regional, national and sometimes international role in England's history, and will continue to shape the area's future.

What gives the area its character?

Landscape is all around us and people are central to how we understand it. Landscape is shaped by, and helps to shape, people's lives. It has been defined as

> an area, as perceived by people, whose character is the result of the action and interaction of natural and/or human factors ... [and which] covers natural, rural, urban and peri-urban areas. It includes land, inland water and marine areas ... [and] might be considered outstanding as well as everyday or degraded [and is an] essential component of people's surroundings, an expression of the diversity of their shared cultural and natural heritage, and a foundation of their identity.[1]

Landscape character is formed by the things that make an area unique, created by a particular combination of components. It is not fixed but is altered over time by people and environmental fluctuations. The character of a landscape is largely created by its history, the types of activities and events that happened there and how they were or are perceived, and physical aspects such as its landforms, geology and soils. These factors affect the components of a

Figure 1
The Hoo Peninsula looking east towards the chimney of Grain power station. The village of High Halstow can be seen in the middle distance and the estuaries of the Thames and Medway in the far distance to the left (north) and right (south), respectively. The former Hundred of Hoo railway, now a goods branch serving the Grain industrial area, is visible snaking through the intensively farmed landscape along with a chain of pylons extending from Kingsnorth power station.
[26474/032]

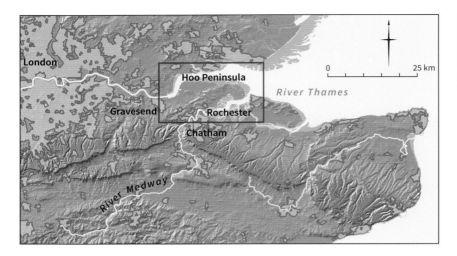

Figure 2
The unique character of the Hoo Peninsula has been
heavily influenced by its location in the Thames Estuary,
30 miles east of central London between the towns of
Gravesend, Rochester and Chatham, and bounded by
the River Thames to the north and west and the River
Medway to the south and east.

landscape such as the types of buildings, shapes of fields, patterns of road networks, local soils and amounts of woodland found in a particular area. Therefore landscape, and not just the particular buildings or monuments that sit within it, has its own heritage value, because it embodies an area's past and will shape its future.

Shaped by ancient rivers

Local topography (or landforms), geology and soils have contributed to the character of the Hoo Peninsula. They have influenced how different parts of it have been used over time, such as how people farmed, where they chose to live and where they established industries. These aspects of the landscape are not fixed but change at varying rates over time, through either natural processes or repeated alteration and adaptation by local inhabitants over many generations.

The changing routes of the Thames and Medway rivers, as well as the effects of ice ages on land and sea levels, have been fundamental in shaping the topography of the area. The rivers appear to have followed completely separate courses until around half a million years ago, when glacial ice forced the Thames southwards to meet the Medway, which at that time flowed across the area of today's Hoo Peninsula into Essex. The rivers eventually merged and moved southwards to their current position. Evidence of the changing routes of the Thames and Medway survives in the form of gravel deposits and can help us understand how the rivers shaped the peninsula. These early sediments also preserve plant and animal remains, which can tell us about the wider environment at the time they were deposited.

Today, a ridge of predominantly London Clay forms the peninsula's central spine of low hills, though Cretaceous chalk outcrops to the west. Clay also underlies the marshland river deposits and, as with the chalk, is overlain by patches of the sand and gravel deposited as the rivers changed their routes over hundreds of thousands of years. More recently, the two rivers in their current positions have deposited silts and clays (in which sand, gravel and peat seams are found) over the extensive marsh areas (Fig 3). The central ridge of higher ground reaches a height of around 100m above sea level towards its

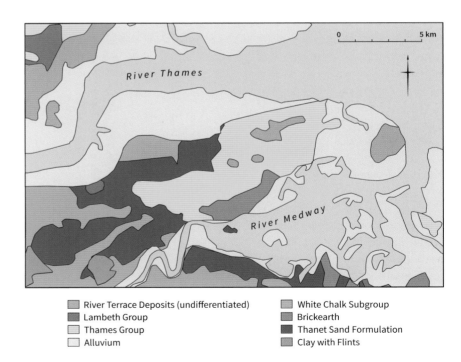

Figure 3
Geology has played an important role in shaping the Hoo Peninsula. London Clay (Lambeth Group and Thames Group) and Cretaceous chalk (White Chalk Subgroup) form the central ridge of low hills, surrounded by alluvium deposited by the rivers running through the area.
[Contains British Geological Survey materials © NERC 2011]

River Terrace Deposits (undifferentiated)
Lambeth Group
Thames Group
Alluvium

White Chalk Subgroup
Brickearth
Thanet Sand Formulation
Clay with Flints

south-western end at Shorne. It forms rolling low hills in the south and east towards the Medway, but to the north and west the ridge drops away more sharply, giving way to much flatter terrain towards the Thames. These topographic differences have helped to create a more exposed landscape facing the Thames and a more sheltered one on the Medway side of the ridge, combining with many other factors to give each side of the peninsula a distinctive character.

As well as contributing to the character of the landscape, the area's distinctive topography also influenced its name. Traditionally thought to mean 'spur of land', the earliest recorded use of the Saxon word 'Hoo' on the peninsula dates from the 7th century, but may refer to the settlement of Hoo St Werburgh or to the distinct heel-shape of the ridge of hills (a recent interpretation of the origin of the word 'Hoo'[2]) rather than to the whole of the peninsula as we understand it today. It is not clear when the term 'Hoo Peninsula' originated but it is probably a relatively modern expression. By the time of the Domesday survey in 1086, the central part of the peninsula was known as the 'Hundred of Hoo', a 'hundred' being a Saxon administrative area, but it is uncertain when the name 'Hoo' came to signify the whole peninsula. By the 17th century travellers and diarists may have been using 'Hoo' more broadly to refer to this part of the north Kent coast, including the Isle of Grain.

The modern landscape

The Hoo Peninsula can be divided into two broad zones based on the nature of today's landscape: the central band of higher ground and low hills running south-west to north-east along its length, and the extensive low-lying reclaimed marshland and salt marsh which surround the higher ground on three sides (Fig 4). To the east, the once separate Isle of Grain is now joined to the main peninsula and forms part of the marshland landscape. Although varied, the two zones each have distinct characters which reflect the interplay of the landscape's physical aspects and how people have used and adapted them.

It is important to remember that neither of these broad zones exists in isolation, and each has influenced the character of the other and contributed to the daily experience of the peninsula's inhabitants. In the medieval period people

Figure 4 (opposite)
Looking south-east across Cliffe Marshes towards the distant ridge of low hills which makes up the spine of the Hoo Peninsula. The marshland and the higher ground form two broad landscape zones.
[DP141623]

used both the higher ground and the marshes as part of a mixed farming regime. Movement between these areas on a daily basis influenced the field patterns and routeways we see today and is also reflected in the inclusion of both types of landscape within most parishes.

The central ridge of higher ground

The central ridge of higher ground forming the peninsula's spine is a landscape of mostly large modern fields predominantly used for arable farming (Fig 5) with a mix of slightly acidic, moderately fertile, loamy and clayey soils.[3] Much of its present appearance originated in the 20th century, when smaller fields were combined to create larger ones and villages expanded considerably. Interspersed within the large fields are three main areas of woodland (Chattenden, Northward Hill and Shorne) and areas, particularly on the northern and western sides of the peninsula, where patterns of older fields from the pre-modern, and in some cases medieval, periods survive. The fields are mainly bounded by grassy baulks, although hedgerows are found on the top of the ridge, where they may have been easier to establish away from the maritime climate. The scattered remnants of an extensive market garden and fruit industry also survive on the ridge, as well as historic and modern recreational facilities such as golf courses, located to the south and west close to the larger Medway towns.

Most of the peninsula's 34,000[4] residents live in settlements which, with the exception of Grain, occupy the central higher ground rather than the marshland, and this has necessarily influenced the character of both areas. The settlements include villages and farmsteads scattered in the wider landscape, their locations

Figure 5
The central ridge of higher ground, predominantly used for arable farming, is the most extensive type of landscape on the Hoo Peninsula.
[DP172033]

influenced by historic patterns of farming. Some settlements are situated close to the transition between the higher ground and the marshes, demonstrating the importance of access to both landscape zones in past farming regimes. Individual farm buildings, particularly on the northern side of the peninsula, also demonstrate the historic importance of providing shelter for animals on or near the marshes.

Today's villages vary greatly in size, from Cooling, with just a few hundred residents, to Hoo St Werburgh, which has nearly 9,000 people living within the parish,[5] and like many other villages in the area has seen the construction of planned post-war housing estates (Fig 6). These estates have altered the historic character of the villages, vastly increasing their size and extending the impact of industrial development beyond the installations themselves. Although this landscape has seen much change, where the earlier historic appearance of the peninsula's villages survives it is expressed through layout, density and continuity of building types as much as historic building stock. Cliffe has many historic buildings, but Cooling and St Mary Hoo have retained more of their earlier historic character due to their unexpanded nature and rare survival of village farms, avoiding the predominance of 20th-century building types and materials seen in some other settlements (Fig 7).

Where they do survive, the oldest buildings on the peninsula are either timber-framed or, in the case of high-status buildings like Cooling Castle and the parish churches (with the exception of the late 19th-century brick church at Upnor), use Kentish Ragstone. Due to the lack of good local building stone, this was probably transported down the Medway from quarries around Maidstone or other sources on the Lower Greensand geology. A few churches, including St Helen's, Cliffe, combine ragstone with flint. However, brick and plain roofing tiles dominate the settlements, having been used extensively from the Victorian period into the 21st century for terraced housing, civic buildings, schools, local authority housing and private housing, the architectural details of the latter often echoing earlier traditional styles.

The different characters of the Thames-facing and Medway-facing halves of the peninsula are also reinforced by the less-developed nature of some of the northern settlements, such as Cooling and St Mary Hoo. This probably reflects past differences in transport links and the relative accessibility of the 20th-century industrial areas and Medway towns from villages on the south

Figure 6 (opposite)
Hoo St Werburgh, the largest settlement on the peninsula, has changed since the Second World War as a result of the construction of large, planned housing estates, such as the Kingshill Estate. These cater for local industrial workers and people commuting to the Medway towns. The historic village core is located between the church and the main crossroads.
[26476/27]

Figure 7 (right)
Some villages, such as Cooling, preserve their historic character and scale. Their location away from the peninsula's main transport corridors has discouraged expansion and reduced pressure to convert village farm buildings to domestic use. Cooling Castle, dating from the 14th century, can be seen in the foreground.
[26598/002]

side of the peninsula. There are exceptions to this, however; for example, Upper Stoke retains a traditional feel despite its Medway-facing location, due to the fact that main transport routes bypass the village.

The central ridge is dominated by east–west routeways which rose to prominence in the 20th century with the development of the Grain industrial area. This area is served by the railway goods branch (*see* Fig 1) and the A228, the peninsula's main road link to the A2. However, the historic significance of this east–west corridor is also demonstrated by the highway hamlets found along these routeways, particularly the Ratcliffe Highway, which may reflect a former droving route. The network of smaller roads on the higher ground generally has a north–south or northwest–southeast alignment, reflecting the former importance of access to now abandoned river connections to the north and south of the peninsula, which would have provided passage across, as well as along, the river.

The marshland and rivers

The estuarine situation of the Hoo Peninsula dominates its character through its views, transport connections and economic and leisure activities. Around a third of the area is coastal marshland. This comprises low-lying marshes reclaimed from the sea and protected from the tide by river walls, much smaller areas of unreclaimed salt marsh beyond these walls and expansive mud flats, exposed at low tides. The estuaries act as both extremely important routeways for waterborne traffic and barriers to land-based movement away from the peninsula. They are intertwined with the peninsula itself, which provides navigational day marks and mooring points for river users. Active commercial and industrial jetties survive only at Grain, Kingsnorth and Cliffe, giving connections to the major shipping routes, and very little cross-river transport persists, although locations such as Hoo Marina and Lower Upnor are a focus for leisure sailing.

Much of the reclaimed marshland, with its moderately fertile loamy and clayey soils,[6] is grazing pasture for inland farms. Its appearance reflects a historic pattern of land use, being divided up by creeks and drainage ditches which vary in their regularity. The scale of the modern sea wall makes it easy to forget the past importance of river connections through the marshes. Footpaths may be the last survivors of routes through the marshes to the rivers. As well as old river walls made redundant by their modern replacement, a scattering of low mounds survive, some from medieval salt production and some built to provide flood refuge for grazing livestock. The Thames and Medway marshes have different natures: the Medway coast feels more sheltered and contains small islands of reclaimed land and scattered fragments of its once extensive salt marsh (Fig 8).

Military and industrial developments in the 19th and 20th centuries changed the marshland. Industry now dominates some areas, although, as we will see, its impact on the character of the marshland is perceived to be much greater than its actual footprint. The largest industries, such as the British Petroleum oil refinery, have now closed, leaving as much of an imprint on people's mind as the landscape itself. The construction materials used in these industrial and military developments, including large volumes of steel, concrete and aluminium sheet, differ greatly from the traditional building materials used on the peninsula. The vertical scale of some of the industrial structures, such as Grain and Kingsnorth power stations, contrasts sharply with the low-lying

Figure 8
The sheltered estuary of the River Medway has a different feel to the broad, open River Thames which sweeps around the northern side of the peninsula. In the Medway, fragmentary salt marsh, islands and the remains of jetties and hulks reflect the differences in both the nature and usage of the two rivers.
[26600/023]

terrain and the scale of other activities taking place, such as farming. Industry has had a greater impact on the character of the Medway marshes than the Thames, as the larger, taller 20th-century industry is focused on this side of the peninsula and the Isle of Grain, in large part due to better transport links and the Medway's deep channel, which allows large ships to dock (Fig 9). Good road and rail links have sustained the only surviving industrial presence on the northern, Thames side of the peninsula at Cliffe, although views of distant industrial activities across the Thames in Essex, such as Tilbury power station and the Coryton oil refinery, reinforce the sense of an industrial landscape even here (Fig 10).

Figure 9
Once separated from the rest of the Hoo Peninsula by
Yantlet Creek, the Isle of Grain is now a focus for
modern industrial activity.
[26866/017]

Figure 10
Views of distant industrial facilities in Essex, on the
north bank of the Thames, serve to reinforce
perceptions of the Hoo Peninsula as an industrial
landscape.
[DP172008]

Same place, different perceptions

Our understanding of landscape character can influence and be influenced by our perceptions. A landscape can be regarded and valued in many ways depending on the interests, understanding and experiences of the observer (Fig 11). How we understand and appreciate the Hoo Peninsula today reflects our own era and particular circumstances. Different individuals or groups may have had different attitudes to the landscape and its value at the same or different times, not least because it is constantly evolving. While it is therefore inevitable that the peninsula will never have a single, clear identity, some common impressions of the area are evident, particularly in written accounts. These focus almost exclusively on the marshland areas, rather than the higher ground, and often originate from outsiders looking in, suggesting that they regarded the marshes as the distinguishing feature of the peninsula (Fig 12).

Figure 11
Our impressions of a landscape are formed in many ways, influenced by images, written descriptions, changing weather conditions and what we know about its history. Our experience of places such as Cliffe Marshes (seen here looking south-west towards Tilbury power station) may reinforce or contradict our impressions depending on the light and weather conditions.
[Rebecca Pullen]

Many writers, from William Lambarde in *A Perambulation of Kent* (1570) to Peter Ackroyd in *Thames: Sacred River* (2007), describe the marshes in melancholic and marginal terms, such as 'uninhabited', 'desolate', 'wild' and 'eerie'. These impressions may have originated from ideas that the peninsula was an unhealthy place, put forward by writers such as William Camden in *Britannia* (1607), possibly influenced by the severe flooding that the area suffered in the 16th century,[7] or by the increasing prevalence of malaria in the marshes around that time (Fig 13). This notion of unhealthiness may have been reinforced in the first half of the 18th century when ships were quarantined in the Medway during outbreaks of plague in Europe. At the same time, however, the marshland environment was considered beneficial to the health of the livestock that grazed there.[10] Historical references to crime on the peninsula include sheep theft, robbery and smuggling. A perception of lawlessness was reinforced by Charles Dickens' decision to hide the convict Magwitch in the marshes in his book *Great Expectations* (1861), perhaps drawing on reports of escapees from the Medway prison hulks heading for the peninsula in 1810.[11]

The idea of the empty marshes surfaces many times in historical and modern accounts and seems to have extended to the whole of the peninsula, particularly in descriptions by 18th-century writers such as Daniel Defoe and Edward Hasted. Although now often viewed in a positive light, as an inspiration or source of spiritual enlightenment, this notion of emptiness may have resulted in a number of negative uses for the peninsula in previous centuries, such as the use of the Medway Islands and Stangate Creek for plague quarantine, the City of London's 1822 decision to reopen Yantlet Creek to the passage of ships, thereby destroying the local road access to the Isle of Grain, and the dumping of London's refuse on the peninsula prior to the First World War.[12] These schemes are all telling of perceptions held by people living beyond the peninsula, often unfamiliar with the area. They persist today, even though the Hoo Peninsula is far from an empty landscape.

Impressions of emptiness or remoteness may have influenced planning and acceptance of industrial development on the peninsula, suggesting a landscape that was practical, appropriate and acceptable for unsafe, noxious or unsightly activities. Negative views of this industrial development became another recurring theme of the area, particularly in the post-war period when the arrival of British Petroleum's oil refinery on Grain appeared to threaten its rural character, although in reality heavy industry had already arrived in some parts of the peninsula over a century earlier. The spread of industry along the Thames in the 20th century, which coincided with an increasing appreciation of the countryside, was seen by some as an unwanted intrusion in an unspoilt natural landscape. The perceived impact of industry on the undeveloped marshes may well have hastened the establishment of the area's nature reserves and protected habitats. Despite negative associations, the peninsula's industrial landscapes have been valued by many for providing jobs and even for their distinctive appearance (Fig 14). Today parts of the landscape are developing a 'post-industrial' character as increasing numbers of retirees move into the area and the peninsula fosters a developing leisure industry, including horse riding and stabling.

By understanding the history of the peninsula's landscape we can set some of these ideas in a broader context. The marshland, with its banks and ditches, is an altered landscape which provides a more understandable context for later industry if, rather than thinking of it as natural, we acknowledge its important economic role as grazing marsh in the medieval period and the capital invested to reclaim the salt marsh from the sea. Although the marshes encompass the smaller part of the peninsula today, the central ridge of mainly arable farmland

Figure 13 (opposite)
Perceptions of the healthiness of the Hoo Peninsula have varied over time. In the 18th century Defoe and Hasted suggested that no families of any status lived there due to its unhealthy nature.[8] Fear of malaria, which was endemic in the area, persisted into the 20th century, when personnel who had previously contracted the disease were banned from working at Kingsnorth airship station.[9] Yet by the 1930s the healthiness of the area was being favourably compared to London's cramped conditions in promotional literature for the planned resort at Allhallows-on-Sea.
[John Minnis Collection]

Figure 14
Despite some negative perceptions of the Hoo Peninsula's industrial landscapes, many people have valued their economic benefits. Their otherworldliness provided inspiration for a 1970 episode of the science-fiction television series 'Dr Who', filmed here at the former Berry Wiggins oil refinery site at Kingsnorth.
[DP172026]

has played a less significant role in how people view the peninsula, possibly because the distinctive marshes dominate the panoramic views. The former importance of Hoo St Werburgh as a Saxon religious centre, known as a minster, also highlights how the significance of a place changes over time.

Investigating landscapes

The Hoo Peninsula is an ideal location for investigating how past activities contribute to landscape character and help to shape what individuals think and feel about the places where they live, work and spend their leisure time today. Continuing a pattern seen throughout its history, the peninsula is likely to see high levels of landscape change in the future through housing development, economic growth and major infrastructure projects. Historic England undertook a major project to investigate how the history of the peninsula is reflected in its landscape, and how a better understanding of this history and its role in shaping the character of the peninsula can make a positive contribution to future change. The project was influenced by the European Landscape Convention, which places these principles at its core and aims to promote the management, protection and planning of landscape for future generations.[13]

Landscape can be investigated in many different ways. We often learn more by combining different kinds of research. The Historic England project brought together different types of landscape-scale research and used a range of specialists to produce an integrated understanding of the development of the Hoo Peninsula's landscape, rather than one focused on a particular aspect or theme. Techniques included review of the peninsula's palaeoenvironmental data, analysis, interpretation and mapping of archaeological sites and landscapes visible on aerial photographs, mapping and interpreting the historic character evident in the modern landscape, seascape and farmsteads (Fig 15), assessing the peninsula's buildings, detailed investigation of some key historical sites (Fig 16) and synthesising the valuable information that has been produced by previous researchers.

This book uses the project results to summarise how the history and archaeology of the Hoo Peninsula have contributed to its distinctive landscape character and sense of place. It explores three themes that have shaped and

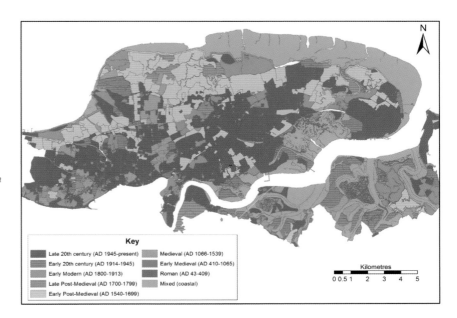

Key

Late 20th century (AD 1945-present)	Medieval (AD 1066-1539)
Early 20th century (AD 1914-1945)	Early Medieval (AD 410-1065)
Early Modern (AD 1800-1913)	Roman (AD 43-409)
Late Post-Medieval (AD 1700-1799)	Mixed (coastal)
Early Post-Medieval (AD 1540-1699)	

Kilometres
0 0.5 1 2 3 4 5

Figure 16
The Historic England project has involved both desk-based research and fieldwork. Here, an investigator records the concrete foundation for a gun battery built at Lower Hope Point, Cliffe in 1900 and now stranded on the Thames foreshore.

continue to shape the modern landscape: i) industry, ii) warfare and iii) farming and fishing. It shows how the peninsula's location, transport links, physical characteristics and military neighbours have enabled it to play important regional, national and international roles in some of these activities.

Information on how to access further project results, in the form of reports and digital data, can be found at the end of this book.

Industry has made the most recent contributions to the character of the Hoo Peninsula landscape. The open terrain, raw materials and transport links provided by the Thames and Medway rivers made the peninsula attractive for a wide range of industries, as part of a general movement of industry along the Thames away from London in the 19th and 20th centuries. Many industries were concerned with new technologies such as electricity, new communications such as radio, and new materials or substances such as oil, chemicals and Portland cement. Together, these innovations may be regarded as a second 'industrial revolution', and their impact on the area was significant. Large expanses of marshland were built over (Fig 17) and the landscape dramatically altered through the excavation of raw materials.

At the same time, many of the peninsula's villages expanded considerably as they accommodated the growing workforce. In the later 19th century smaller, often terraced, housing was built for incoming workers, along with new Nonconformist chapels to cater for their spiritual needs. From the late 1950s large housing estates were built for workers at the oil refinery and power stations using non-traditional concrete designs known as the Cornish Unit Type 1 and Airey systems (*see* Fig 34). The legacy of industry varies across the Hoo Peninsula and evidence of very early industries such as Roman potteries and salt works is now buried under the marshes. Not all of the industries established in the 19th and 20th centuries survive, but their remains, whether well preserved or fragmented and overgrown, are testament to the important role the peninsula played in the modernisation of England.

Salt from the sea

Figure 17
British Petroleum's vast Kent Oil Refinery, during construction in the early 1950s. The village of Grain can just be made out towards the top right of the image, dwarfed by the refinery. Over 1,000 construction workers were housed in a nearby purpose-built camp during this period. For some people the refinery's arrival established the Hoo Peninsula's predominantly industrial character.
[Aerofilms EAW045776]

The boundary between land and sea is blurred by the rough grassland of the salt marsh that fringes the peninsula. The salt marshes, unprotected by sea walls, are regularly flooded by the high tide, creating a brackish landscape, and it is from here that salt can be obtained. The importance of salt as a food preservative has ensured a long history of production in the area, although evidence from many periods is largely hidden from view. Excavations have uncovered pottery that suggests salt was being made as early as the Bronze Age[14] and have also revealed the brine tanks, hearths and waste mounds associated with Roman salt making.[15]

Although little documentary evidence survives, many grass-covered mounds dotting the marshland are formed of medieval salt-making waste and thus provide evidence of salt production on the Hoo Peninsula in this period. Construction of sea walls for land reclamation cut off the tides and contributed to the demise of the medieval industry. Salt making returned, perhaps as early as the 16th century, when salt pans were established on the Isle of Grain, possibly hoping to exploit the London markets. These works were relatively small, unable to meet even local demand, and were eventually abandoned during the first half of the 19th century.[16]

Building materials

The peninsula's natural resources of clay, chalk and gravel ensured that it was well placed to capitalise on the huge demand for building materials created by the 19th-century growth of London and nearby towns such as Rochester and Chatham. These resources were exploited by existing industries such as the peninsula's brickworks, which expanded as a result (Figs 18 and 19). By the early 19th century the Medway brickworks were producing hundreds of millions of bricks for both residential and industrial buildings[17]: in 1844 one works in Frindsbury produced over 14 million bricks – 1 per cent of the nation's total output at that time. Hoo St Werburgh had a number of brickmakers, including the Hoo Brick Company, Wilson Brothers and Hoo Lodge Brickworks, which produced bricks of a deep red colour.[18] The peninsula's natural resources were also used by the new Portland cement industry. Portland cement, on its own and as an ingredient of concrete, is one of modern Britain's characteristic building materials, and the chalk and clay found on the peninsula attracted cement works near the Thames at Cliffe (Fig 20) and on the Medway at Frindsbury. The clay from both river estuaries was generally considered to produce the best Portland cement and the Thames and Medway area became the centre of Britain's Portland cement industry in the second half of the 19th century, selling cement both at home and abroad.

The brick and cement industries were in decline by the early 20th century, although brick making continued at Hoo St Werburgh until the mid-20th century and cement manufacture at Cliffe until 1970[19]; gravel processing still

Figure 18
The remains of one of Hoo St Werburgh's brickworks, photographed in 1952. The riverside location of the works demonstrates the importance of the river for transporting the finished bricks. A tramway was used to deliver the clay from the more distant clay pits, and this was washed and then allowed to dry out in the washbacks seen near the top of the photograph. Some of the buildings below these may be moulding sheds where the bricks were formed, while the open area between the washbacks and the coast is where the bricks were laid out to dry.
[RAF 58/856 4178-9 14-Apr-1952]

Figure 19
The brickworks site is now occupied by Hoo Marina Park. Comparison of this photograph with Figure 18 shows how the brickworks influenced the layout of the park.
[PGA Tile Ref: TQ7771/7871 21-APR-2007. Aerial Photography: Licensed to Historic England for PGA through Next Perspectives™]

Figure 20
The remains of chamber kilns built at Cliffe cement works at the end of the 19th century. They were probably intended to replace the earlier bottle kilns and satisfy an increasing demand for building cement. [Sarah Newsome]

Figure 21
The cement manufacturer Francis & Co provided some accommodation for its workforce around Cliffe. This photograph shows Cliffe Ville, formerly the Royal Albert public house, with numbers 1–5 Concrete Cottages beyond. The Royal Albert originally occupied the eastern end of a terrace, Cliffe Villa Cottages, which in 1881 was home to 19 people, including 5 cement workers and 1 engine driver. The grandest house built by the company was for the foreman of the works, but this no longer survives. [DP172032]

Figure 22
The fragmented remains of Stoke Saltings, with Kingsnorth power station in the background. A huge quantity of clay was removed from the salt marsh in the 19th century, dramatically changing the coastline. The mud was dug by labourers called 'muddies' and taken by barge to the cement works further up the Medway.
[DP165032]

continues today. Relatively little survives of the cement and brick works, but later 19th-century housing built to accommodate the workforce forms part of their legacy (Fig 21). The greatest impact of these industries on the Hoo landscape can be seen where the raw materials were extracted. Large quarry pits, now water-filled, survive at Cliffe, while on the Medway the extraction of millions of tonnes of clay for the cement industry resulted in the almost complete removal of the salt marsh between Hoo St Werburgh and Grain (Fig 22).

Transport connections

The cement and brick industries made extensive use of the rivers for transport. Clay was loaded onto barges beached on the salt marsh, for delivery to the cement works, and both finished bricks and cement were distributed by river. An attempt at improving river communications saw the creation of the 11km-long Thames and Medway Canal, which opened in 1824. It linked the two rivers by cutting across the western end of the peninsula between Gravesend and Strood, allowing vessels to avoid the long voyage around the coast. This included the construction of the 3.5km- (3,946yd-)[20] long Higham Tunnel (which was later split in two by digging down to create a passing place).

Figure 23
Abandoned boats like these near Hoo St Werburgh reflect the decline in smaller vessels using the rivers.
[DP172027]

Although river transport remains fundamentally important to some industries on the Hoo Peninsula, it declined during the 20th century due to the contraction of the cement industry and competition from the railways. This was reflected in the reduction of the number of barges on the rivers (Fig 23).[21] The preference for rail during the 19th century is clearly illustrated by the history of the Thames and Medway Canal, which in the 1840s was largely filled in and part overlain by a railway, a conversion which included reuse of the canal tunnel (Fig 24).

Improved rail links were established in the late 19th century when a line was laid along the peninsula to the Isle of Grain. Initially requested by local farmers to improve access to markets for their produce, the line was built by the South Eastern Railway to serve a new rail and ferry port for Atlantic and continental traffic. The line was laid in 1882 to the new facility named Port Victoria, which consisted of a pier, hotel and station (Fig 25). This venture was not successful and much of the site was redeveloped during the building of the British Petroleum refinery in the 1950s. The railway infrastructure, which eventually brought new industry and military activities to the area, continues in use today and now connects to the container port which opened in the 1990s close to the site of the 19th-century port (*see* Fig 1). A branch line was also constructed to the speculative seaside resort of Allhallows-on-Sea in the early 1930s, and while the town never flourished, its legacy survives in the form of Allhallows Holiday Park, with its wooden chalets and caravans (Fig 26).

Figure 24
Higham railway station was built close to the northern end of Higham Tunnel, whose mouth can be seen in the background of this photograph dating from c 1885. Originally dug for the Thames and Medway Canal, it is a noteworthy example of a railway reusing a canal tunnel.
[John Minnis Collection]

Figure 25
A short journey from London (38 miles) was seen as the main advantage of Port Victoria, seen here c 1910, when it opened with an ultimately unfulfilled aspiration to become an intercontinental passenger terminal. Located at the mouth of the Medway, it provided relative privacy for European royalty visiting Britain and became a favoured embarkation point of Queen Victoria.[22]
[John Minnis Collection]

Figure 26
The attempted creation of a new seaside resort at Allhallows-on-Sea in the early 1930s emphasised the healthy environment of the local area and the ease of access to London provided by the specially constructed railway branch line, now closed, which served the new resort. Though much of the development was never completed, the size of some buildings, such as the British Pilot public house, reflects the extent of its original aspirations.
[DP165123]

Explosive activities

The open and sparsely populated nature of the marshland made it particularly suitable for potentially dangerous activities, and gunpowder storage magazines were built on St Mary Marshes and Cliffe Marshes in the 1890s, both utilising the Thames for transport. In 1900, under the new ownership of Curtis's and Harvey Ltd, the Cliffe site expanded rapidly, producing a wide range of the new chemical explosives that were superseding gunpowder, including nitroglycerine-based explosives such as cordite. Patented in 1889, cordite is a smokeless propellant that provides higher velocities and greater ranges than gunpowder. The variety of explosives produced at Cliffe placed the factory at the forefront of explosives technology and in 1908 it was described as 'one of the largest in the kingdom'.[23] The factory exploited its Thames-side location with specially constructed jetties which enabled it to import raw materials produced further along the Thames, transport finished products and access test facilities and shell-filling factories. Large amounts of water were also necessary for the explosives production (Fig 27).

As with the nearby cement works, many of the factory's workers lived in Cliffe and, although the explosives factory was a smaller employer, some new houses were built for its workers, including the manager, as well as a second school for the growing number of children in the village. Working at the explosives factory was dangerous and the human cost of numerous accidental explosions is illustrated by some of the gravestones in Cliffe's churchyard.

At its fullest extent the factory comprised 300 structures and occupied 128 hectares. The organic layout of the earlier western part of the site respects the marshland landscape, in contrast with the regular arrangement of the eastern side built during the First World War. Laid out under government control in 1916 and known as HM Cordite Factory, the eastern side was designed to help meet the Royal Navy's need for cordite during the war. The inevitable reduction in demand for explosives when the war ended resulted in the factory's closure around 1920. The completeness of the surviving factory remains is remarkable and they mark Cliffe's brief role in a global war with a seemingly insatiable appetite for ammunition (Fig 28).

Figure 27
The Curtis's and Harvey Ltd chemical explosives factory
was an industrial works of national importance. The
company was attracted to the peninsula by a number
of factors, including ease of access to London and
international shipping routes via the River Thames,
and open, flat land away from settlements.
[26866/47]

Figure 28
HM Cordite Factory formed part of the extensive
explosives works of Curtis's and Harvey Ltd. This
photograph shows the remains of the acetone recovery
buildings in the foreground and extending off to the
right, with cordite blending houses in the distance on
the left.
[DP141667]

Transatlantic communication

The topography and location of Cooling Marshes attracted innovative 20th-century transatlantic radio communication technology (Fig 29). One of the world's most complex short-wave radio receivers was built there by the Post Office in 1938. The marshes offered an ideal environment for the radio station:

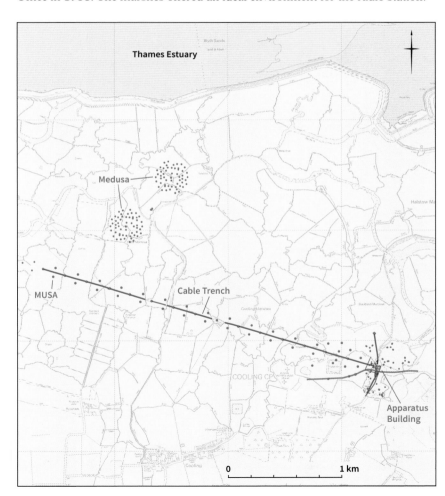

Figure 29
Cooling Radio Station consisted of a main apparatus building connected via cables laid along a trench (marked in green) to a series of diamond-shaped (rhombic) antennas along its length (marked as red dots); each antenna was 60ft (18.29m) high. The two clusters of red dots to the north are the antennas of an experimental short-wave receiving station known as Multiple Direction Universally Steerable Aerial System (MEDUSA), which was in place by 1961.
[© Crown Copyright and database right 2015.
All rights reserved. Ordnance Survey Licence number 100024900]

open, flat land for its antenna system which extended out for two miles (3.2km); a three-mile forward clearance to the river (necessary as sea walls could disturb the radio waves); and saline waterlogged ground to produce the highly conductive conditions needed for successful operation, all while being close to London. Building on the marsh was challenging and the main building required a foundation of 150 concrete piles, each 24m deep, in order to prevent it from sinking. This station had a steerable receiving antenna array (known as MUSA – Multiple Unit Steerable Antenna) which was designed to overcome the problem of fading signals that occurred when radio waves, divided in transmission, cancelled each other out at the receiver. The array pointed towards the source of the signals, which were transmitted from Lawrenceville, New Jersey, USA, while signals from Britain were transmitted from Rugby in Warwickshire and received at Manahawkin, New Jersey. Testing was interrupted by the outbreak of the Second World War but the station eventually became operational in 1942. The MUSA array system was the last major technological development of the short-wave radio communication era, representing the ultimate short-wave receiving system. The site was closed in 1965, superseded by satellite and transatlantic telephone technology. Although the antennas have been removed, the partially demolished apparatus building survives.

Oil refining

Oil is a key industrial product of the 20th century and has done much to shape our modern world, not only in terms of the various fuels and lubricants produced, but also for its role in the petrochemical industry. Most of Britain's crude oil is imported by sea and the peninsula's undeveloped marshland adjacent to the deep-water berths offered by the River Medway made it an ideal location for the establishment of oil storage and refining. Some of the earliest British oil refineries were established on the peninsula between the two World Wars and Britain's post-war expansion of domestic refining capacity included the creation of the huge British Petroleum complex built on the Isle of Grain in the 1950s.

Oil first arrived on the peninsula in 1908 when fuel tanks were erected by the Admiralty on the Isle of Grain for the purpose of refuelling the Royal Navy's new oil-fired vessels (Fig 30). These tanks reflected an increasing demand for oil

Figure 30
Part of the Admiralty fuel oil station established on the Isle of Grain in 1908, photographed in 1950 and since demolished. Oil offered great advantages to the Royal Navy: compared to coal-fired vessels, oil-fired ships were faster, could be refuelled at sea and were less likely to be spotted as they produced less smoke. The decision to adopt oil was somewhat contentious as, unlike coal, there were limited domestic supplies and thus Britain's naval capability became reliant on foreign fuel.
[RAF 540/393 PO20-23 30-Jul-1950]

in the early years of the 20th century, both as fuel for ships and for road vehicles. As a result oil began to challenge coal's dominance as Britain's main source of fuel. Although very little crude oil was refined in Britain during the first half of the 20th century, two refineries were established on the peninsula at Kingsnorth and on the Isle of Grain.

In 1923 the Medway Oil and Storage Company (MOSCO) refinery was built close to the Admiralty site (Fig 31). This was one of the few independent companies operating between the World Wars, and it marketed its fuel under the name Power Petrol. MOSCO ceased refining in the 1930s but in 1931 Berry Wiggins & Co opened a refinery at Kingsnorth, which primarily produced bitumen (Fig 32). In 1937 they opened Bees Ness Jetty in order to exploit the deep-water channel and in 1995 it was still recorded as the longest in Britain at 2.5km (Fig 33).[24] Other oil storage was established on Grain, including tanks built during the Second World War which were buried under mounds of soil in an attempt at camouflage.

A major programme of post-war refinery building in the United Kingdom was prompted by the increasing demand for petroleum products.

Figure 31 (left)
The Medway Oil and Storage Company (MOSCO) refinery on the Isle of Grain, photographed in 1925. Elements of this site were later incorporated into the 1950s British Petroleum refinery.
[Aerofilms EPW013202]

Figure 32 (opposite, above)
The Berry Wiggins & Company refinery at Kingsnorth photographed in 1935. The refinery was built on the site of the naval airship station and reused a number of its buildings. The site is now largely demolished but the refinery's jetty survives in a derelict state (see Fig 33).
[Aerofilms EPW047584]

Figure 33 (opposite, below left)
The Berry Wiggins & Company's Bees Ness Jetty stretches across Stoke Saltings and Stoke Ooze and is thought to be the longest jetty in Britain. A more modern but shorter replacement jetty can be seen in the background, heading for Kingsnorth power station.
[27196/024]

Figure 34 (opposite, below right)
A rare example on the peninsula of an unclad Cornish Unit Type 1 house, in Hoo St Werburgh. Prefabricated concrete systems were sometimes used for large estates constructed in the post-Second World War period as the houses were quick and easy to build. Concrete panel systems were also used to construct the shopping parade in Hoo St Werburgh and the village halls at Cliffe and Grain.
[DP172144]

British Petroleum began building the huge Kent Oil Refinery on Grain in 1950. This involved realignment of the road across Grain and major landscape changes: the filling-in of fleets and channels and the alteration of the coastline including the enclosing of a bay to create a reservoir. As with other industries, new houses for the expanding workforce were built across the peninsula, partly as a consequence of the failure of a 1950s scheme co-sponsored by British Petroleum for a new town at Allhallows (Fig 34). Occupying almost a third of the Isle of Grain, by 1964 the Kent Oil Refinery had become the second largest oil refinery in Britain. Its output helped to meet Britain's increasing oil consumption, which rose from 10 million tonnes in 1946 to 103 million tonnes by 1970.[25] However, rising oil prices in the 1970s led to a dramatic drop in consumption and the Kent Refinery was eventually closed as part of a European-wide reduction in refining capacity in the early 1980s.

Generating electricity

Perhaps most prominent of all the peninsula's industrial sites are the massive power stations built by the Central Electricity Generating Board (CEGB) at Kingsnorth (construction of which began in 1963) and on the Isle of Grain (begun in 1971). Power stations have been a notable feature of the Thames riverside close to London since the late 19th century, but the creation of the National Grid in the 1920s allowed new stations to be built further from centres of consumption. The Hoo Peninsula provided the open and sparsely populated areas where it was then considered reasonable to build large power stations, while the rivers provided the essential cooling water required by these stations, as well as access for fuel deliveries (Fig 35). Oil was seen as a cheap and convenient alternative to coal and the Thames and Medway estuaries were also home to a number of refineries. Kingsnorth was designed to burn both coal and oil but the shift towards oil is most clearly seen on the Isle of Grain where the power station was entirely oil fired and supplied by the neighbouring British Petroleum refinery (Fig 36).

Once completed, Grain power station was claimed to be 'the largest oil-fired power station in Europe' and Kingsnorth was 'the largest dual-fired power station in Europe and the only example in Great Britain'.[26] The huge size of these power stations reflects the increased output made possible by technical advances in boiler and generating unit design. The electricity generated was transmitted

Figure 35
Kingsnorth power station and its jetties on the Medway, which were used for coal and oil deliveries. The design of this station utilised the shape of the coastline: cooling water taken from the Medway by the main buildings was discharged via Damhead Creek to the left of the station, from where it flowed back to the Medway, re-joining the river 3km downstream. It is now closed and in the process of demolition.
[Detail of 26477/011 8-Sep-2009]

Figure 36
Grain power station, whose construction was overseen
by architects Farmer & Dark Ltd, was intended to burn
oil from the adjacent British Petroleum refinery. Its
construction was beset by industrial disputes and its
completion in 1982 coincided with the closure of the
refinery. Though architecturally impressive, its use was
limited by high oil prices. It is now closed and in the
process of demolition.
[DP165048]

via the pylons that cross the peninsula, but Kingsnorth also had a direct link to London via an experimental underground transmission system that connected one of its generators to the capital. The application for another entirely oil-fired station at Kingsnorth submitted in 1974 demonstrates the perceived suitability of this landscape as a location for these large power stations. This proposed station was never built and by the end of 1975, facing the threat of higher oil prices, Kingsnorth was converted to burn more coal.

Environmental concerns have led to more stringent limits on pollutant emissions and without modification Grain and Kingsnorth power stations have now reached the end of their operational lives. A proposal to replace Kingsnorth in 2008 met significant public opposition on environmental grounds and both stations are now closed and under demolition. They represent some of the last of the monumental power stations and will be replaced not by similar-sized plants but by small lower-output, gas-fired stations such as those already present on the peninsula.

Military activity made significant contributions to the character of the Hoo Peninsula landscape from the 14th century onwards. Threats of war have been the impetus for a variety of military surveys and the subsequent establishment of defences on the Hoo Peninsula (Fig 37). The peninsula's position between the Thames and Medway rivers meant that many of these defences were concerned with the protection of London and of Chatham, used as a naval dockyard from the 16th century. During the 19th and 20th centuries the Royal Navy's presence extended beyond the dockyards at Chatham and nearby Sheerness and a number of naval facilities were built on the peninsula. The magazines at Chattenden and Lodge Hill and the fuel oil storage on Grain all directly served the fleet. The Admiralty was also responsible for Grain Island Firing Point near Yantlet Creek, used for testing ordnance, and, with the development of air power, the creation of two air stations for the Royal Naval Air Service (RNAS) on the peninsula and the Marine Aircraft Experimental Depot on Grain. The influence of the peninsula's military neighbours also affected the development of the village at Upnor. Its high street, running down to the river and terminating at the castle, reflects the settlement's special relationship to the dockyard in the 17th and 18th centuries (Fig 38).

Figure 37 (opposite)
In response to French raids along the River Thames during the Hundred Years War, potential landing grounds on the Hoo Peninsula were surveyed and fortified in 1380–1 by a commission headed by John de Cobham. Around this date, Cobham built Cooling Castle, purportedly to protect the local area; the copper plate set into the gateway (shown here) states that the castle was 'made in help of the country'. Cooling's defensive capabilities have been questioned, but the castle and its inscription are nevertheless symbolic of the long history of defensive works established on the peninsula.
[DP165131]

Figure 38
Upnor's High Street, with its weather-boarded late 17th- and 18th-century buildings, is orientated towards Chatham Dockyard, which had a significant influence on the development of the settlement during this period. A ferry operated across the Medway between Upnor and the dockyard from at least the 18th century.
[DP172450]

Initially established at Lodge Hill just before the First World War, anti-aircraft batteries reflected the continuing importance of the peninsula in defending both the capital and the naval installations concentrated around Chatham. Although the peninsula's coastline is largely unsuitable for a land invasion, the position of 19th-century forts at Allhallows-on-Sea and Grain reflects vulnerable points, as do the remains of the Second World War anti-invasion defences on the coast and further inland. The continual development of new weapons, ships and aircraft determined the design and armament of each generation of defences, as well as their location, alteration and ultimate abandonment. Many of the obsolete sites no longer survive but those ruins still present in the landscape serve as a reminder of the important role the Hoo Peninsula played in defending the country.

Coastal defence

The first purpose-built coastal artillery fort on the Hoo Peninsula was Higham Blockhouse, built on the south bank of the Thames around 1539–43 in response to the threat of foreign invasion following Henry VIII's break with Rome. It was one of five new forts established on the Thames downstream of Gravesend and Tilbury. Together they guarded the approach to the capital and were part of a wider programme of coastal defences built in the south of England during this period.

Higham Blockhouse was short-lived and the building was demolished in 1558, but a new fortification was built on the Medway riverside at Upnor with the express purpose of protecting naval vessels anchored in the river. Work began on Upnor Castle in 1559 and with various modifications it continued in this defensive role until 1668 (Fig 39). The defence of Chatham was supplemented by smaller gun emplacements known as 'sconces' built downstream of the castle, which no longer survive, and the provision of a boom chain across the river to act as an obstacle to ships (Fig 40 and *see* Fig 44).

These defences proved insufficient during the Second Anglo-Dutch War (1665–7). In 1667 Dutch ships raided the Medway and, after landing troops and destroying the fort at Sheerness, broke through the boom chain, sailing as far as Chatham where they destroyed and captured Royal Navy ships. A subsequent review of the Medway defences led to the abandonment of Upnor Castle and the

Figure 39
Upnor Castle was built between 1559 and 1567 during
a period when angled bastions were being introduced
into fortification design, a feature that became
characteristic of defences well in to the 19th century.
Upnor's design only follows a partial bastion plan,
with a single example projecting into the river.
[26886/039]

Figure 40
Both World Wars saw the reintroduction of defence
booms around the peninsula. This photograph shows
part of the boom across the Thames at St Mary's Bay.
The wooden structure ran across Blyth Sands for
1.24km, with wire nets covering the remaining
distance to Canvey Island.[27] On the peninsula there
was a small camp and generator powering
searchlights on the boom that could illuminate the
river; on the Essex side there was a coastal battery.
[Detail of RAF TQ7978/1/1416 S412H54 17-Aug-
1941]

creation of a new line of defence further downstream designed by the noted military engineer Sir Bernard de Gomme. This consisted of a fort at Cockham Wood (Fig 41), the ruined remains of which are still visible on the riverside, paired with a fort on the opposite side of the river at Gillingham. New batteries, probably no more than temporary gun platforms, were also built further downriver on islands such as Hoo Ness, Oakham Ness and Bishops Ness, and on the Isle of Grain. These were relatively short-lived and by the late 18th century, despite the presence of the fort at Sheerness, the Medway was considered by the Royal Engineer Hugh Debbeig to be poorly defended.[28]

No new permanent defences were provided on the Medway side of the Hoo Peninsula during the French Revolutionary Wars (1792–1802), but this conflict did provide an impetus for the construction of two new batteries on the Thames at Shornemead and at Lower Hope Point.[29] These were part of a national programme of fort construction and were intended to support the existing forts at Tilbury and at Gravesend. Their location echoed the distribution of the 16th-century blockhouses (Shornemead was around 1km upriver of the location of Higham Blockhouse) and, like those earlier defences, the new forts were short-lived and were abandoned after the Napoleonic Wars ended in 1815.

From the middle of the 19th century fear of French aggression sparked the so-called 'three panics' (1847–8, 1851–3 and 1859–61). During the first of these the fort at Shornemead was demolished and replaced with a new defensive

Figure 41
The remains of Cockham Wood Fort on the northern bank of the Medway. Built in 1669, originally for 44 guns, it is one of a sequence of defences constructed on the peninsula to protect the nationally important naval dockyard at Chatham, and the later garrison. [DP114021]

structure, completed in 1853. This was the first of a new design of polygonal forts to be built in Britain that did not use angled bastions and towers. Concerns raised by the final of the three panics, alongside rapidly developing artillery technology and an expanding French navy with iron-clad, steam-powered warships, led to the setting up of a Royal Commission on the Defence of the United Kingdom in 1859. The recommendations of this commission initiated an intensive and costly programme of fort construction across the country, intended to prevent a French invasion.

The Royal Commission was responsible for many of the fortifications still visible on the Hoo Peninsula today. These new forts had substantial stone casemates with steel shields and shutters designed to withstand naval bombardment and were grouped to provide crossing fire with other forts. The fort at Shornemead was again replaced and a new fort was also built at Cliffe (Fig 42); these could cross fire with each other and with a third new fort at Coalhouse (on the site of an earlier fortification) on the Essex side of the river. As well as supporting these two forts, Shornemead was intended to be the first in a line of fortifications overland towards Chatham, although this was never

Figure 42
Built in the 1860s, Cliffe Fort was one of three forts constructed where the Thames turns northwards downriver of Tilbury and Gravesend. An arc of granite-faced casemates fronted the river, with barracks to the rear. It remained in use as a battery until the 1920s and served as a base for the Royal Navy Auxiliary Service during the Second World War.[30]
[26474/020]

constructed. Slough Fort was built downriver at Allhallows where it could defend this vulnerable point on the peninsula against enemy landings. The entrance to the Medway was defended by Grain Fort and Grain Battery, which could cross fire with Sheerness. In the Medway an inner line of defence was provided by forts on the islands of Darnet Ness and Hoo Ness (Fig 43).

All of these Royal Commission forts were completed by the 1870s, but some were disarmed from the early 20th century when it was concluded that London could be adequately protected by the long-range guns at the batteries at Slough Fort, Grain and Sheerness. The First and Second World Wars saw only minor changes to this eastwards movement of coastal batteries. Some sites, such as Grain Fort, continued in use until after the Second World War, but it was only possible for a fort to provide long service with periodic updating of the guns and alterations to the fabric (Fig 44). This was the case for forts such as Cliffe, which was fitted with the steam-winch-powered Brennan Torpedo in the late 1880s, and Slough Fort at Allhallows, where new guns were mounted in wing batteries flanking the original fort in the 1890s. The innovative torpedo installation at Cliffe Fort was one of only eight such facilities built worldwide, reflecting the fort's crucial position defending the route into London (Fig 45).

Figure 43 (below left)
Located on islands in the Medway, Darnet Fort (shown here) and Hoo Fort formed part of Chatham Dockyard's inner line of defence. Their circular design allowed all-round fire. Darnet Fort was used as a battery until the early 20th century and served as an observation post during the Second World War.
[Sarah Newsome]

Figure 44 (below)
Grain Tower, completed in the 1850s, was one of the last gun towers to be built in Britain. It was constructed in the mouth of the Medway to defend Chatham and Sheerness. Despite being considered too small and weak when finished, it was in service until 1910 and again during both World Wars. Later modifications include adjacent barrack accommodation. Part of the iron chain that formed the First World War boom defence across the Medway survives secured to the tower.
[DP165042]

Figure 45
Protecting London from blockade was a key long-term priority of national defence strategy. The innovative Brennan torpedo built at Cliffe Fort in the late 1880s was one of many installations on the peninsula positioned to prevent access to London along the River Thames. The retractable torpedo observation tower which rose from the concrete cone (shown here) was unique and designed to overcome problems caused by the low-lying topography.
[DP097689]

Preventing invasion

Only Allhallows and Grain offer suitable landing ground on the peninsula for invading troops, being located at points where breaks in the extensive marshland give access directly from the coast to higher terrain. This partly explains the positioning of the 19th-century coastal batteries at these two points, but it was during the Second World War that the most extensive anti-invasion defences were established. Both these potential landing grounds were defended with concrete blocks, minefields and barbed wire forming a first line of defence (Fig 46). A second line of defence, in the form of an anti-tank stop line, ran further west between Hoo St Werburgh and Cliffe. Cutting off the peninsula in this way echoed the proposed but never built line of 19th-century forts from Higham to Chatham. Its route partly reflects fears of a German invasion force landing on the peninsula and then making its way towards the capital. The Hoo Peninsula stop line formed the northern section of the Newhaven–Hoo General Headquarters (GHQ) Line that ran from the Sussex coast to the Thames. This in turn was part of a national network of stop lines put in place during the invasion

scare of the summer of 1940. The Hoo stop line consisted of a ditch for most of its length, although in some places it incorporated features such as woodland and quarries that would present sufficient obstacle to tanks. Infantry and artillery pillboxes, gun emplacements and roadblocks were placed along its line. These linear inland defences were soon abandoned in favour of mobile defence and the creation of small defendable areas.

Supplying the fleet

The stop line also provided protection for the naval magazines at Chattenden and Lodge Hill. These magazines were among a number of sites on the peninsula that served the Royal Navy. The need to store increasing quantities of ammunition had accelerated over the centuries due to the number of conflicts that the navy was involved in, the growth of the fleet, the introduction of new forms of ammunition and the increased demands of quick-firing guns. The earliest magazines were located close to the Medway. Upnor Castle was

Figure 46
Most of the peninsula's Second World War anti-invasion defences have been removed but some have survived, such as these concrete anti-tank obstacles on the beach at Grain.
[DP172139]

converted to a magazine after the 1667 Dutch raid, but by the 1760s it was too small and a nearby storehouse was converted as a temporary magazine. The castle was still in use as a magazine by 1812, even after a new magazine with a capacity of 10,000 barrels had been built to the north towards Lower Upnor. After the Crimean War (1854–6) a shell store and another magazine with a capacity of 23,000 barrels were built, completed in 1857.[31] Although additional stores and facilities were constructed at this site well into the 20th century, no space remained for bulk storage. In 1877 work commenced on five new magazines to the north of Upnor in Great Chattenden Wood (Fig 47). Chattenden was soon dwarfed by the nearby Royal Naval Ordnance Depot at Lodge Hill, which was under construction in the late 1890s. Lodge Hill consisted of magazines, filling sheds and a laboratory and occupied 125 hectares. A railway

Figure 47
The naval magazines at Chattenden. Each magazine could hold 4,000 barrels of gunpowder and was set within a substantial earthwork traverse.[32] Situated approximately 2km from the Medway, they and the nearby Lodge Hill depot were connected to Upnor by a railway.
[26475/032]

linked these sites to Upnor and the main railway network, making Lodge Hill the first ordnance depot in Britain that could be supplied without the need for sea transport.[33]

War in the skies

The Hoo Peninsula has a long association with the Royal Navy and coastal defence. The development of airships and aeroplanes in the early years of the 20th century introduced the threat of aerial bombardment in any future conflict. This raised specific concerns about air raids on naval magazines and cordite factories but also fuelled fears that London might be attacked. In response to these fears anti-aircraft guns were positioned on the peninsula at Lodge Hill and Beacon Hill in 1913[34] to defend the magazines at Chattenden and Lodge Hill (Figs 48 and 49). These were Britain's first permanent anti-aircraft emplacements and over the course of the war other sites, including Cliffe explosives works and Chatham Dockyard, were defended by anti-aircraft

Figure 48
The remains of one of the two earliest permanent anti-aircraft batteries in Britain, built at Lodge Hill in 1913. A gun was fixed within each of the circular emplacements either side of the central ammunition store (see Fig 49). To the right is a blockhouse and on the left a defensible war shelter providing accommodation for those operating the battery.
[Detail of 27951/014]

Figure 49
An artist's impression of the First World War anti-aircraft gun battery at Lodge Hill when in use, showing the defensible war shelter in the foreground and the two gun emplacements either side of the ammunition store.
[Peter Dunn]

batteries on the peninsula. The peninsula's location east of London also meant that these guns could be used against raiders heading for the city and so ensured that even in the new era of air warfare the peninsula would continue its long tradition of defending the capital.

The anti-aircraft batteries on the Hoo Peninsula were abandoned after the First World War, but the deteriorating political situation during the 1930s saw their reintroduction as part of the Thames and Medway Gun Defended Area, which contributed to the defence of London. During the Second World War some of these batteries were modified to take more powerful guns and some additional batteries, including a Z battery of rockets at Lodge Hill, were built. During the summer of 1944 the number of guns on the peninsula was significantly increased when batteries were rapidly deployed to engage the V1 flying bombs.

Defence from air attack was also provided by aircraft and at the end of 1912 a Royal Naval Air Service (RNAS) seaplane station, the first of a series of coastal air stations designed to defend ports, was established on the Isle of Grain to defend the naval dockyards at Chatham and Sheerness. The RNAS was the

Royal Navy's airborne arm, which alongside the British Army's Royal Flying
Corps was tasked with developing new flight technologies for military purposes.
The two organisations merged to form the Royal Air Force (RAF) in 1918. The
fiercest part of what the *Chatham, Rochester and Gillingham News* characterised
as the 'first aerial battle that has ever taken place over British soil' occurred in the
skies above the peninsula on Christmas Day 1914. Described in official sources
as having a seaplane bottom, a German biplane headed up the Medway and then
across the peninsula towards London while attempts were made to intercept it
using anti-aircraft guns and British aircraft, including one from Grain air
station.[35] Aircraft had also been used for other operations and by 1913 a second
RNAS base had been established at Kingsnorth, allowing airships easy access to
the Thames and English Channel in order to fly anti-submarine patrols (Figs 50
and 51). This was the only operational airship station at the start of the First

Figure 50
*Airship hangars photographed during the 1920s
following the closure of the naval station at Kingsnorth.
The original timber roof structure of one of the hangars
has since been reused in an agricultural building at
Moat Farm in St Mary Hoo and is protected as a
listed building.*
[Detail of Aerofilms EPW047581]

Figure 51
Despite the site's later reuse as part of the Berry
Wiggins oil refinery, a few smaller buildings from
Kingsnorth airship station survive within a modern
industrial estate, including the red-brick building in the
centre of this photograph and the building opposite with
the black (replacement) roof. Airships were a key
component in safeguarding the nation's coastal
shipping lanes during the First World War.
[27200/12]

World War. The Admiralty's existing land ownership and the lift-gaining advantages of being close to sea level with few hills and suitable prevailing winds may have been additional factors in the station's establishment on the peninsula.[36] Both air stations closed in the 1920s but at the start of the Second World War a civilian airfield at Gravesend was requisitioned by the RAF and planes flew from there during the Battle of Britain.

During the Second World War attempts were made to protect sites on the peninsula from night bombing by using bombing decoys. A large decoy to protect Chatham was established on Nor Marsh, an island in the Medway 5km east of the dockyard. In addition to electric lights, a variety of structures burnt fuel in such a way as to simulate the effects of an air raid. Another decoy on Cliffe Marshes was to protect RAF Gravesend, while the fuel storage facility on the Isle of Grain had a decoy located on Allhallows Marshes.[37] The fires at this decoy were contained in circular or semi-circular pools which mimicked the actual storage tanks that were located around 3km to the south-east (Fig 52).

Research and development

The local contribution to air warfare around the time of the First World War was not restricted to the anti-aircraft batteries and operational airfields. While anti-submarine patrols were flown from Kingsnorth, the station also undertook the development and construction of airships (Fig 53). Grain air station also had a research and development role in its early years and in 1915 the Port Victoria Marine Experimental Aircraft Depot was established, where a range of planes was developed, although none went into mass production. One of Grain's innovations allowed aeroplanes to make emergency landings at sea and stay afloat.[38]

In 1917 the Admiralty also requisitioned marshland on the Isle of Grain and from the following year the War Office developed Grain Island Firing Point for the testing of artillery. This site operated as an 'out' battery of the experimental establishment at Shoeburyness on the Essex coast. Guns were delivered by rail or river via Yantlet Creek and very large shells were test-fired across the Thames estuary to Maplin Sands in Essex, giving the range a total length of 27km. Grain's unique geographical relationship with Maplin Sands and the military test firing range at Shoeburyness, Essex, meant that shells could be retrieved from the soft sands or shallow water in a manner not possible at the country's other test facilities.[39]

Figure 52
The remains of the bombing decoy on Allhallows Marshes. Set on top of the lines of drainage ridges are two circular channels within irregular earth banks which form firebreaks. The channels would be supplied with fuel and lit to replicate burning oil tanks, with the intention of drawing enemy bombs away from the real oil installations to the south.
[27960/016]

Figure 53
Some of the officers, men and women at the Royal
Naval Air Service's Kingsnorth station in 1918. At the
outbreak of war in 1914 there were over 200 members
of staff.
[OP04536]

Changing approaches, lasting legacies

From the 1920s, with the closure of the airship station at Kingsnorth and the experimental station on Grain, the Grain Island Firing Point was the only remaining site associated with research and development on the Hoo Peninsula. The testing of ordnance there eventually ended in the 1950s. The short-lived existence of some military sites is not unusual and reflects the ever-changing nature of threat and the means to defend against it. The reduction in the number of operational coastal batteries on the peninsula from the early years of the 20th century was significant, yet at roughly the same time the area was witnessing the introduction of Royal Navy air stations and anti-aircraft batteries. These new sites reflected the 20th-century threat from air attack and also indicated the peninsula's continued importance in national defence. However, by the 1950s the advent of nuclear weapons had made both coastal and anti-aircraft artillery redundant. Not only was defence no longer being undertaken at a local level, but the installations in need of defence were closing too. Both the nearby Royal Navy dockyards were closed before the end of the 20th century, Sheerness in 1960 and Chatham in 1984. Some of the military sites on the peninsula have now been largely cleared but the remains of others survive. With the area's long history of defending Chatham Dockyard and London it is perhaps fitting that the most prominent remains are of the 19th-century coastal forts overlooking the Thames and the Medway.

Figure 54
Local authority housing was first built on the peninsula in the wake of the 1919 Housing Act, which provided local authorities with subsidies to build more accommodation for working people. Housing stock was often named after national military heroes, for example Kitchener Cottages at Lower Stoke (shown here), after the army general. Local military connections also seem to have been honoured in this way. Beatty Cottages in Allhallows and Jellicoe Cottages in High Halstow are named after naval figures and Trenchard Cottages in Grain were named for the first head of the RAF, reflecting the village's role in early aviation.
[DP165038]

The military presence in the peninsula has also left other varied legacies. Some military structures have been reused for other purposes (*see* Fig 50) and remnants of the temporary accommodation known as Bungalow Town survive on Grain. Local military connections may have influenced decisions to name housing built on the peninsula during the inter-war period after First World War naval and RAF figures in particular (Fig 54). The concentration of large numbers of troops in the area seems likely to have influenced the construction of concrete embarkation points known as 'hards' at Upnor and Shornemead Fort during the Second World War, to allow for the embarkation of landing craft and troops for the D-Day landings. Finally, the overall development of the villages of Upper and Lower Upnor have been heavily influenced by historic military connections, including the presence of the castle, the ordnance depot and the proximity of Chatham itself.

4

Farming and fishing

As we have seen, in the last few centuries military activities and industrial developments, particularly those on the Medway marshes, have been important in shaping the character of the Hoo Peninsula. However, people have been adapting and managing the peninsula and its estuaries through fishing and the farming of crops and livestock for thousands of years and farming continues to transform the landscape today. The varied and changing nature of farming activities has been influenced by patterns inherited from earlier farmers as well as the peninsula's location, topography, geology and soils.

Exploitation of resources such as wildfowl (Fig 55), fish and shellfish also has a long history on the peninsula, but has left a subtler imprint on the landscape. The estuaries have provided resources throughout the peninsula's history and the Thames and Medway rivers have long been important fisheries, with fishing rights recorded for manors on the peninsula in the Domesday Book of 1086 (Fig 56). Cliffe was a medieval fishing port, with a quay and a crane in the mid-15th century,[41] although its form and history are poorly understood, and a small fishing industry existed at Avery in Allhallows parish after the medieval period. Shellfish such as mussels, and particularly oysters, were important until the 19th century when all fishing in the area declined due to poor weather, pollution and over-exploitation. Artificial pits of unknown date surviving on the salt marsh around the peninsula may represent piecemeal attempts to revive the shellfish industry.

Figure 55 (opposite)
The decoy pond on the marshes at High Halstow illustrates one way that people have exploited the Hoo Peninsula's natural resources. Decoy ponds were introduced from the Netherlands in the 17th century. Wildfowl landed on the pond (now overgrown) and were lured to the ends of the attached, originally netted channels, known as pipes, where they were caught. Though decoys survive in other parts of the country, this is the only example known to survive in the county of Kent.
[27949/019]

Figure 56
The London Stones at Upnor are two of a series of stones which were erected at various dates in the 19th and 20th centuries to formally mark the limits of the jurisdiction of the City of London on the Thames and Medway rivers. From as early as the 13th century this jurisdiction gave London authorities control over the rivers' important fisheries and the right to collect tolls. Another stone survives at the mouth of Yantlet Creek, on the north side of the peninsula.[40]
[DP165026]

Early farmers

Farming has shaped the Hoo Peninsula landscape for at least 3,000 years, although people may have been living there for a much longer period. We have greater evidence for, and therefore a better understanding of, farming from the medieval period onwards. Where evidence for the peninsula's early landscapes and their occupants survives it is mostly buried beneath the modern land surface. Chance finds and excavated material indicate very early (Palaeolithic) human activity on the peninsula, as does evidence from the wider region, such as the important human skull fragments and flint tools from around 400,000 years ago found at Swanscombe, 10km to the west.[42]

Evidence from archaeological excavations, such as pottery from Allhallows,[43] suggests that by the end of the Neolithic period (around 4,500 years ago) people were settling on the peninsula. Buried ring ditches, recorded across the area as cropmarks on aerial photographs, probably indicate the position of late Neolithic or early Bronze Age barrow mounds (Fig 57). Although generally associated with burial, these monuments may also have marked

Figure 57
Two ring ditches near Lower Stoke, visible from the air, where the crops have grown and ripened differently over the buried ditches. They probably indicate the location of mounds (now removed) used for late Neolithic or early Bronze Age burials, which often also mark important places in the prehistoric landscape, such as routeways or boundaries. The other patterns in the field reflect natural variations in the underlying soils and geology.
[26976/021]

important routes or boundaries in the landscape. Aerial photographs and archaeological excavations, for example at Damhead Creek and Malmaynes Hall Farm,[44] have revealed buried evidence that from around the middle Bronze Age (3,500 years ago) prehistoric people were dividing areas of the peninsula into ditched enclosures linked by trackways. These suggest mixed farming practices where it was necessary to move animals between arable fields (Fig 58). Excavation of oyster shells and cereal grains from Middle Stoke suggests that both marine exploitation and farming were taking place by this period.[45]

Evidence of how people lived and farmed on the peninsula through the Iron Age, Roman and early medieval periods (roughly 2,800 years to 1,000 years ago) survives in the form of buried remains and, for the early medieval period, some early documents. Long before the Norman Conquest in 1066 people had

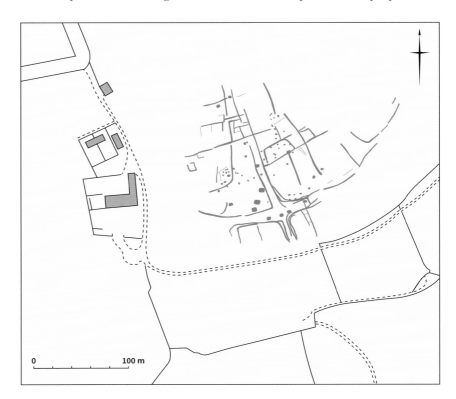

Figure 58
Small areas of enclosures and trackways in Cooling parish, revealed on aerial photographs as patterns produced by differences in crop growth over buried ditches. These could be of any date from the prehistoric through to the early medieval period and may relate to settlement, agriculture and the management of livestock.

0   100 m

established an agricultural regime involving arable cultivation, stock husbandry and fishing, which still influences the character of the landscape today. This mixed farming economy is reflected in the position of the present settlements, which were established, probably in the early medieval period, in order to exploit both land and coastal resources. The pattern and nature of the peninsula's settlements and fields today reflect how generations managed these resources in response to their own needs and to local and distant markets.

Reclaiming tidal salt marsh

The Hoo Peninsula's salt marsh was important for grazing and the exploitation of estuarine resources such as shellfish and salt. After – and possibly even before – the Norman Conquest, landowners on the peninsula began constructing walls and drains to reclaim the salt marsh from the tides, creating enclosures (Fig 59). This had a lasting impact on the landscape. Historic documents record reclamation activity on the Hoo Peninsula from the late 12th century to the early 15th century. However, a doubling of the values of the manors of Cliffe, Cooling and Chalk between 1066 and 1086 is notable and may indicate new landlords and bishops improving their estates via reclamation at this earlier date.[46] A dramatic increase in manor values was not recorded in the Medway parishes in the same period. This could indicate that some land here had already been reclaimed by wealthy pre-conquest landowners, such as the Bishop of Rochester, or that the Medway parishes, with their higher proportion of arable land to marsh, had less to gain from reclamation. It also suggests a long history of differing character between the Medway and Thames marshes.

Reclamation (sometimes known as 'inning') was undertaken in order to improve the productivity of the salt marsh. In addition to protecting land from the impact of flooding, inning also created nutrient-rich pasture which could sustain a larger number of animals and provide valuable fodder or higher cereal yields. These benefits increased rents and profits, boosting the value of manors and enabling post-conquest lords to reinvest in their new estates and reinforce their status. Reclamation was an expensive activity dominated by wealthy church establishments, but it was also undertaken by individual landowners, although fewer records of their endeavours survive. The benefits of reclamation

Figure 59 (opposite)
Reclamation, the process of building walls to enclose and then drain and subdivide areas of tidal salt marsh, began around the 12th century, or possibly even earlier, and was one of the most important processes in creating the landscape of the peninsula that we see today. Through reclamation wealthy landowners could increase the value of their land as, once reclaimed, it could sustain more animals, provide fodder crops and produce higher cereal yields.
[26866/034]

are demonstrated by the effort needed by landowners to maintain the long river frontage on the Hoo Peninsula compared to the relatively small area of reclaimed marsh it actually enclosed.[47]

The loss of land to tidal inundation via breaches in the sea walls was common in the medieval period, particularly on the Isle of Grain. The current pattern of walls and ditches probably dates mainly from the early 17th century and originated during a period of rebuilding and re-inning after severe flooding in the 16th century.[48] The complex medieval reclamation process is hard to reconstruct as the subsequent floods may have wiped out many earlier boundaries, making documented medieval marshes difficult to locate in the modern landscape. Although some walls have been fossilised within later areas of reclamation, as on Cooling Marshes, others may have been dismantled to provide earth for new walls, and if re-inning was undertaken in one swathe, then earlier evidence for incremental medieval reclamation and wall-building may have been lost. Reclamation had a greater impact on some parishes than others: the Isle of Grain was completely transformed as nearly all of its field enclosures originate from marshland or salt marsh. Whatever the details of the process, reclamation changed the Hoo Peninsula dramatically: reclaimed marsh and salt marsh now constitutes a third of its area.[49]

The patterns and form of enclosures within the peninsula's reclaimed land reflect a number of factors and need further detailed study, as does the relationship between pastoral activities and the salt production mounds on the marshes, which undoubtedly changed as reclamation reduced access to the volumes of sea water needed for this form of salt production. The process also changed how people moved around the marshes and perhaps in some places, like Cliffe, cut off routes to the sea (Fig 60). However, large areas of Stoke Saltings were not enclosed, possibly due to the fisheries located there, and this has helped to create the different characters of the Medway and Thames estuaries that we see today. Networks of paths and livestock refuges recorded in the 19th century, which show how the unenclosed salt marsh was used and its historic value for grazing, hint at the impact of inning on these landscapes (Fig 61). Salt marsh in the Thames estuary used for grazing had been eroded by the river by 1800 and by the mid-19th century it had been largely removed by the mud digging for the Portland cement industry on the Medway side of the peninsula as well.

Figure 60 (opposite)
An extract from George Russell's 1695 map 'A Plot of Cliffe Level' showing the termination of a number of routeways (including the Ham and Farthing 'Walls') as they head north into the marshes beyond Cliffe village. The points at which the routeways end may represent the former limits of the tidal salt marsh before more reclamation was undertaken to the north, changing how people accessed these areas and the coast.
[KHLC S/NK/P/8a, Kent History and Library Centre, Maidstone]

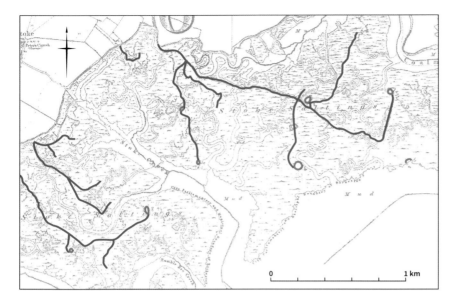

Figure 61
The routeways (highlighted in blue) and livestock
enclosures or refuges (shown in red) recorded on this
map of Stoke Saltings from 1870 help us to understand
how the salt marsh was valued and used historically,
and the impacts of reclaiming these important grazing
areas.
[Base map © and database right Crown Copyright and
Landmark Information Group Ltd. All Rights Reserved
2015. Licence numbers 000394 and TP0024]

Medieval farming

Medieval farming in north Kent involved intensive arable agriculture combined
with grazing livestock on the reclaimed marshes. Production was intensified by
leaving less land fallow than in other medieval farming regimes and by growing
fodder crops for animals. The sheep and cattle that grazed the Hoo Peninsula
marshes were used to fertilise the arable fields on the higher ground from the
medieval period until the 19th century, either by moving them on to the fields
at night or redistributing manure (Fig 62). In the medieval period ecclesiastical
landowners took up new farming techniques in parallel with their reclamation
efforts, expanding sheep production on the marshes and keeping arable
production high. The earliest reference to farming in Cliffe relates to intensive
sheep rearing on the marshes.[50] A flexible regime, with land farmed individually
rather than communally, and the proximity of the London and European
markets, seems to have bolstered land values through various market collapses
in the medieval period.[51] Unlike the rest of the country north Kent continued to
produce large quantities of grain in the late 15th and 16th centuries because it

Figure 62
The practice of grazing sheep on both reclaimed and unreclaimed marshes before moving them on to higher ground at night to manure arable stubble or fallow fields was a key part of the medieval farming regime, and surviving records document this practice on the peninsula.

supplied these markets. The large church in Cliffe could be seen as a reflection of the wealth generated in the parish by farming and fishing in this period.

In medieval Kent gavelkind tenure, where inherited land was divided between all sons rather than passed to just the eldest, resulted in farmers holding arable parcels scattered through many fields, rather than just a few main ones around a village.[52] As land was shared out, new dwellings were constructed in some of these scattered parcels,[53] meaning that medieval farmers were more likely to live in farmsteads and hamlets dispersed throughout the fields, rather than in villages. The resulting patterns of land ownership meant that farmsteads were sited in relation to scattered rather than ring-fenced holdings and that some land within a parish would be held by people who didn't live there, as tithes for Higham from 1841 show, for example.[54] This pattern appears to have been typical across the peninsula, suggesting that its land was valued by people living further afield.

Many farmsteads were positioned on the edge of marshes to allow exploitation of the marsh grazing, although on the Isle of Grain farmsteads were located on the marshes themselves due to the limited amount of higher ground. The modern marsh-edge Eastborough Farm and Bromhey Farm in Cooling were originally included within a detached part of Frindsbury, a parish located to the south of the peninsula, highlighting the value of access to this landscape.[55] Farmsteads in most parishes had farm buildings (outfarms) on the marshes to provide shelter and storage. Medieval documents record cow houses, sheepfolds and sheep wicks (probably comprising barns with some form of domestic accommodation), and maps from the late 17th and early 18th centuries depict numerous small buildings which probably reflect some continuation of the medieval pattern of individual holdings on the marshes.[56] The use of outfarms varied from parish to parish: there were few outfarms on Allhallows Marshes compared to Cliffe Marshes in the 19th century. Shorter distances between the Allhallows home farms and the marshes may have rendered them unnecessary, or the tradition may have died out at an earlier date in the parish. Buildings located in marshland enclosures in the 1950s occupied the same sites as buildings shown on maps from the late 17th century, and although not the same structures, they indicate continuity in the use of this landscape. Even where fields were rationalised by larger farms in the 19th century, new outfarm buildings show a continuing need to house livestock and their fodder in the marshes.

In many places on the peninsula the pattern of medieval farming has contributed to the character of the modern fields, particularly to the north and west where the marshland landscape has seen less change, although even here very straight drains indicate later rationalisation of the more irregular medieval field patterns. In Cliffe, dispersed farmsteads and surviving open (unenclosed) fields at the core of the parish retain elements of medieval character (Fig 63). In common with medieval farming practices across north Kent, the fields around Cliffe were not farmed communally but were divided and farmed by individuals. In other areas, such as at Allhallows and St Mary Hoo, possible groups of medieval strips, consolidated and enclosed to form regular fields probably in the early post-medieval period, appear to survive in the modern field pattern.[57] There seem to be differences between the way the Cliffe open fields were divided (possibly with stones or paling) and the now consolidated field strips in areas of Allhallows, Stoke and St Mary Hoo where low banks (known as leys) visible on

Figure 63
The fields to the south of Cliffe village seem to have changed little since the medieval period. They are open, unenclosed by walls or hedges. In the medieval period these strips of land, or parcels within them, would have been marked out by stones, sticks or fences and farmed by individuals rather than co-operatively.
[DP165134]

aerial photographs may have demarcated strips. Hedgerows were not common on the peninsula and the surviving grassy field boundary banks may also have originated from the practice of farming open strips.

Medieval farmhouses and farm buildings (such as barns) on the peninsula were timber-framed with wattle and daub, reflecting readily available materials and the lack of local building stone. Reeds cut from the marshes were used for thatch, although thatch has now been replaced by plain roofing tile across the peninsula. Some of these farm buildings reflect the wealth of their owners, such as the barn built at Frindsbury for the monks of Rochester around 1403.[58] From the late 17th century, buildings with timber frames were protected from the coastal climate with brick cladding or, in the late 17th to early 19th century, by weatherboarding (Fig 64). Better farm survival on the central ridge means that most early fabric is found here rather than on the marshes, and examples of fine timber-framed houses facing routeways and former open fields survive.

Figure 64
Weatherboarding, such as seen here on the late
16th-century Grade II listed Great Dalham
farmhouse in High Halstow, was added to buildings
on the peninsula from the late 17th century to
protect timber frames.
[DP172146]

Growing demands

By the 18th century the development of the London markets, followed by those of the military towns of Sheerness and Chatham, had led to relative prosperity across north Kent, which was visible in the building, rebuilding or remodelling of farmhouses using red brick in new fashionable styles seen across the country. This included many houses and farmhouses across the Hoo Peninsula from the late 17th century through to the early 19th century, which may have represented their owners' attempts to demonstrate status, wealth and aspirations (Fig 65). Examples include the farmhouse at Mackays Court Farm, Lower Stoke, which was refronted in brick during this period, and the fashionable brick façade at Brickhouse Farm, Allhallows, which was designed to be seen from the road.

Regular, formal planned fields, probably laid out by agricultural surveyors in the 18th and 19th centuries, reflect a reorganisation of farming at this time. However, there also seems to have been remarkable stability in farming and settlement patterns in this period. New farmsteads on the peninsula were not built within these newly enclosed open fields as in some other parts of the

country. Farmsteads with a surviving medieval farmhouse in the hamlet of
Lower Higham and on isolated farmsteads in the rest of Higham parish, indicate
where farmers began the long process of consolidating medieval farming strips
into their own fields and reorganising their farmyards to more modern designs.

Victorian improvements

Although some rare and fragile examples of small barns and cattle housing
constructed prior to the 19th-century agricultural improvements survive on the
peninsula, the 19th century brought many changes to farming regimes and,
subsequently, the landscape. In the mid-19th century farmers moved away from
cereal crops and sheep farming and shifted, on the higher ground at least, to the
production of potatoes, hops, fruit and seed and market gardening on an
industrial scale, exploiting Hoo's excellent transport links and reasonable soils.
Henry Pye, based at St Mary Hoo, pioneered these changes across the peninsula,
alongside general farm improvements, from around 1850 onwards,[59] introducing
extensive drainage across the reclaimed marshland (Fig 66; *see* Fig 52) and
possibly the stock refuge mounds which are found on top of the drainage ridges.
Pye was also instrumental, along with other local farmers, in bringing the
railway to the peninsula in order to transport produce to the London markets
and the continent, influencing military and industrial developments on the
peninsula for the next century.

These 19th-century changes led to much farm amalgamation in order to
create larger farms worthy of the economic investment, and farmsteads were
rebuilt to improve efficiency. The decline in sheep farming meant that many
outfarms were lost at this time as they were no longer needed. The character of
the settlements changed as new farm workers' cottages were built in villages and
on higher ground at the expense of the existing outlying cottages, particularly
those on the marshes, possibly because livestock were being moved less regularly
and labour needs were concentrated in the farmyard instead. The character and
location of the peninsula's modern farmsteads reflects these changes as their
layout embodies their different functions, including storage, processing and
sheltering livestock. The distribution of farmstead types reflects how the medieval
farming patterns have both persisted and been modified on the peninsula.

Figure 66
Narrow parallel ridges, as seen here on Cliffe Marshes, were introduced across extensive areas of the marshland in the 19th century in order to improve drainage and boost productivity.
[Sarah Newsome]

In the 19th century farmsteads with dispersed layouts (comprising two or three working buildings) were replaced with buildings grouped around courtyards. These courtyard farmsteads became the dominant type on Hoo, reflecting intensification and the increasing importance of manure from yard-fed cattle for hops, arable and fruit. Today farmsteads with random arrangements of buildings reflect the earlier, less intensive agricultural regime and are found across the central ridge. By the end of the 19th century many farmsteads with loose courtyard groups had been remodelled into regular courtyard layouts (linked ranges surrounding a yard, often with a detached farmhouse), possibly at the same time as their fields were reorganised, in order to create interlinked, labour-efficient buildings (Fig 67). These types of farms are located in or around villages, perhaps reflecting changing labour needs. The largest and most prestigious multi-yard farmsteads developed around the marshlands, with yards for feeding cattle that also used marshland grazing, but few of these survive.

Figure 67
North Street Farm in Hoo St Werburgh dates from the mid-19th century and is one of a small number of traditional farmsteads on the peninsula that have retained their historic form. Some of the farm buildings, and possibly the farmhouse itself, had been constructed by 1839, but the regular courtyard layout reflects later 19th-century improvements in farmyard design, which responded to the need for farms to become more labour-efficient and produce large quantities of manure from yard-fed cattle for use in fertilising crops in the surrounding fields.
[26888/010]

Farming in the 20th century

The 20th-century shift towards a modern, cereal-based system of farming has also contributed much to the character of the peninsula landscape, bringing changes to fields, farms and villages. Many of the large fields that now dominate the central ridge are the result of 20th-century field amalgamation where field boundaries have been removed in order to accommodate modern farming techniques and machinery. The marshes saw less change in this period and some livestock farming persists today, although the use of the marshes for arable was actively encouraged in the 1970s. Fruit production and market gardening have also declined, although remnants survive towards the western end of the peninsula and some orchards have recently been planted.

As well as contributing to the character of the fields, 20th-century changes in farming have also had an impact on farm buildings. The economics and reduced labour needs of farming in the 20th century brought huge change to the historic farmsteads through farm amalgamation. The traditional farmsteads on the Hoo Peninsula have experienced higher levels of change than elsewhere in Kent and other parts of England where farmstead survival has been mapped: 50 per cent of farms existing on the peninsula around 1900 have either been lost completely or only the main farmhouse survives, no longer occupied by a farming family. A further 20 per cent have lost over half their historic buildings.[60]

This reflects many factors, including an increased redundancy in traditional farm buildings, particularly smaller ones which are harder to adapt to large machinery or to an alternative use, or which do not meet modern animal welfare standards. Barns and oasthouses (used for drying hops) are the buildings most likely to have been converted to other uses (Fig 68) but small farms located in settlement cores and the outfarms and field barns which were so significant in the historic farming regime of the peninsula have been particularly vulnerable to demolition, after being redundant for many years.

A growing population, with many residents commuting beyond the peninsula for work, has helped to drive the demand for conversion. This has been more prevalent on the south side of the peninsula's central ridge due to the proximity of the Medway towns for commuters. This is part of a broader pattern of national change in where people work and live in the 20th century, which saw people moving out of urban areas to 'plotlands' settlements such as Cliffe Woods (Fig 69) in the hope of improving their quality of life, a trend bolstered by the dominance of commuting to work resulting from a dramatic increase in car ownership in the second half of the 20th century.

Figure 68
As farming practices on the peninsula changed during the 20th century, larger barns were more easily converted to other uses. This barn at Cooling Castle is now a venue for weddings and parties.
[DP172014]

Figure 69
Cliffe Woods was originally known as the Rochester
Park Estate and Garden Suburb.[61] *Partially cleared*
woodland was divided into long, narrow plots and sold,
from July 1914, by a private speculator, generally
resulting in self-built bungalows and chalets which
lacked centrally planned services. The estate was
redeveloped in the 1960s but some modern boundaries
echo the original plots.
[Ordnance Survey 25-inch. Kent Sheets XI.6 and XI.10
(revised 1939–40 and 1931). Reproduced by
permission of the National Library of Scotland]

The future of the Hoo Peninsula landscape

The preceding chapters have highlighted the varied history and archaeology of the Hoo Peninsula and how these have contributed to the distinctive character of today's landscape. Far from being a marginal place lacking in historical interest, many of the events and activities that have taken place over the centuries have been part of much bigger stories with national, and sometimes international, significance, particularly in the spheres of industrial, military and technological development. Especially striking is the modernity of many of the activities which took place on the peninsula, with its open, flat land, proximity to London and major military installations and two major river transport routes placing it at the forefront of the development of new technologies such as chemical explosives, powered flight, oil refining, power generation and global communications.

Through these activities the Hoo Peninsula has seen major change and it is certain that change will continue (Figs 70 and 71). New chapters will be written in its history and new layers of interest will be added, during which time the historic character visible in its current landscape might be lost or significantly changed. Conservation of the historic environment is the process of managing change in a way that sustains, and where appropriate enhances, the significance

Figure 70 (opposite)
The Hoo Peninsula continues to change. On the Isle of Grain new industrial activities, like the container port seen here, are replacing older industries such as the oil refinery, whose footprint is beginning to disappear from the landscape.
[26477/027]

Figure 71
Demolition work in progress in the vast turbine hall of Grain power station. The Kingsnorth power station is also in the process of being demolished.
[DP166730]

of a historic place, be it an individual building or monument, or an entire landscape like the peninsula. To be sustainable, change needs to balance economic, social and environmental impacts, while delivering public benefits for each. A key reason for studying the Hoo Peninsula was to ensure that, as the title of this book series implies, decisions about future change could be better informed by an understanding of how the place came to exist, what is most meaningful about it and how this could be affected by change.

All aspects of the peninsula's current landscape have historic character, combining the complex and varied strands of evidence revealed in this book. So that future generations can appreciate this story while making their own contributions to, and forming their own perceptions about, the landscape, it is essential that an understanding of historic character informs decisions on how the peninsula might now evolve. This is not a call for the preservation of the landscape as it is today. Some heritage features or sites are assessed as being special and they have protection that acknowledges their national importance and signals the need for careful consideration of their futures, but value also resides in the more typical and commonplace. As this book has shown, Hoo has been shaped by processes both within and beyond its boundaries, and this will continue in the future. Change has created the distinctiveness of the place and sustainable planning decisions need to recognise the cultural processes that have shaped it. It is not a blank canvas upon which major change can take place without consequences for its historic character and the way that character benefits the people who live, work and spend time there.

Agendas for change

Agendas for change are already at work on the peninsula. Some are development proposals of varying scale but others relate to environmental factors, such as climate change resulting from human activities. The peninsula has recently been rejected as a possible location for a new hub airport (Fig 72) but such ideas are not new and, if ever implemented, an airport, its infrastructure connections and associated ancillary developments would constitute a single change of a magnitude that the peninsula has never seen before and lead to massive transformation. Even without such large-scale change other proposals for

Figure 72
Construction of the proposed Thames Estuary airport
on the eastern end of the peninsula would bring
landscape change on an unprecedented scale.
[© Foster + Partners]

development are significant. It is likely that the existing national role for energy supply will continue at the eastern end of the peninsula with older forms of energy production and storage, such as the out-dated power stations, being replaced. On the redundant ordnance facilities at Lodge Hill a significant new town is proposed whose routeways and plots reflect the layout of the former depot (Fig 73). The development will bring additional residents to the area and thus create new demands on its landscape. This poses some risk of harmful change but also creates opportunities to address existing issues, perhaps transforming perceptions of the peninsula as a sparsely populated area suitable only for unsightly or otherwise unwelcome land uses. Another proposal is for Stoke Harbour, a new garden city of up to 150,000 people focused on the present parish of Stoke, to help alleviate housing shortages.

Future population growth in the Medway towns and north Kent in general will see increasing numbers of people looking for leisure opportunities and other uses from the peninsula. It is likely to become better known and more widely

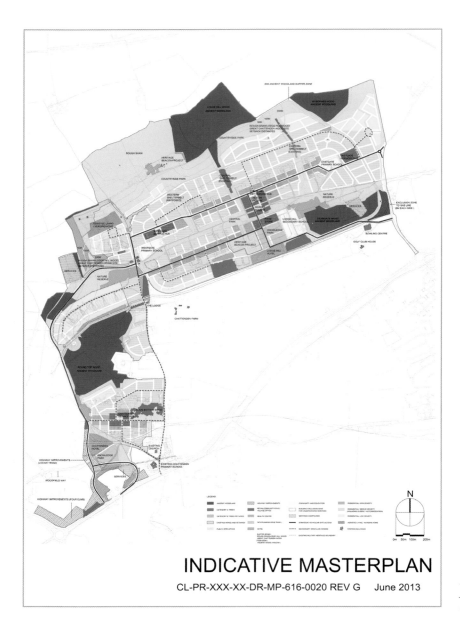

INDICATIVE MASTERPLAN

CL-PR-XXX-XX-DR-MP-616-0020 REV G   June 2013

Figure 73
A plan showing the new settlement proposed for the
former naval ordnance depot at Lodge Hill.
[Courtesy of Land Securities]

appreciated as a landscape to be enjoyed and explored. This creates a need to help people understand the Hoo Peninsula and this book contributes to meeting that need. More visitors to the peninsula might create opportunities to provide new sustainable uses for some of the many buildings and monuments that are known to be at risk and otherwise face uncertain futures. Slough Fort, for example, is being repaired and presented as part of the redevelopment of the existing holiday park (Fig 74).

Environmental change has been a constant factor in the history of the Hoo Peninsula due to its estuarine position. Research on historic sea-level change has demonstrated that the past coastline was very different from today and that marshland reclamation and exploitation from the medieval period onwards have helped form the modern landscape. The Hoo Peninsula is highly prized for the beauty of its natural environment and it contains habitats and populations of fauna and flora that are of international importance. The contribution of past human activity in creating these now valued aspects of the landscape has to be acknowledged, and as a result no part of the place can be considered truly natural. People are attracted to the peninsula for its landscape as a whole and it is fortunate that agendas for change affecting both the natural and historic environment can combine to produce benefits for both. It has to be remembered

Figure 74
Tourism is securing a sustainable future for some historic sites on the peninsula. Slough Fort is being repaired and presented as part of the redevelopment of the adjacent holiday resort (shown here). The resort advertises one of its highlights as being the '19th-century fort offering the best estuary views'.[62]
[26589/040]

that while habitats can to a major degree be recreated, heritage assets are an irreplaceable resource. Services that are derived by communities from the natural environment are sometimes referred to as 'ecosystem services' and rely on a network of 'green infrastructure' such as parks, countryside and footpaths. With careful planning it should be possible to accommodate sustainable change on the peninsula that avoids harm to the environment and enhances its value and the benefits to be derived from its green infrastructure. Joining up the natural and historic environment agendas provides the opportunity for shared and improved outcomes (Fig 75).

Despite the impact of past and present industries on the peninsula, it always was, and largely remains, a predominantly agricultural landscape. Changes in farming practices can be expected to continue, particularly under the influence of climate change, which may further alter the traditional landscape character as new crops or methods of cultivation are introduced. Recent experience has

Figure 75
The flooded pits created by clay and chalk extraction for the Portland cement works at Cliffe now form the Cliffe Pools nature reserve. Many of the peninsula's valuable habitats are the result of human activity.
[DP172019]

Figure 76
Modern sea defences on the foreshore at Grain. Climate change may result in the need to improve or even realign coastal flood defences on the peninsula. [DP172010]

demonstrated the vulnerability of coastal locations to storm events and this is a historic issue for the area. After the major storm of 1953 the flood defences around the peninsula were comprehensively upgraded. It is expected that further actions, to work alongside natural processes rather than controlling them, will be necessary. On the Hoo Peninsula this may lead to realignment of the coastline (Fig 76).

Future research

This book is largely based on archive sources and evidence visible in the landscape, through which Historic England has helped to frame a number of important questions about the history of the peninsula. Visible evidence is strongest for the more recent periods of change such as the creation of medieval and later agricultural landscapes and the impact of industries and defence installations. Much less is known about the organisation of the landscape in Roman or prehistoric times. New investigation of the buried archaeology of the peninsula, by excavation for example, was beyond the project's scope and it remains under-researched and less well understood. New development is likely to require examination of extensive parts of the peninsula and if well handled this will provide the opportunity to learn more about all aspects of its history. Local residents also have much to contribute and their research will enhance understanding of the area for the future (Fig 77).

Figure 77
The military archaeology of the peninsula is a source of much interest. Here, volunteers clear a gun emplacement in the right wing battery at Slough Fort, Allhallows-on-Sea.
[© Victor Smith]

Historic England believes that if we value our past it can enrich our future. Understanding is central to this idea: when people understand the historic environment they are more likely to value it and to look after it so that it can be enjoyed by themselves and others. This means making the history and archaeology of a place relevant in the present day and managing it in a way which delivers wider benefits while ensuring that the majority of the resource can be passed on to future generations so that they too can value it and ask new questions of it. The project on which this book is based was initiated to enhance our understanding of the landscape and will form an improved platform for ensuring its fullest contribution to the future of the peninsula.

Notes

1 Anon 2000

2 Mills 2003, 28; Gelling and Cole 2003, 186

3 http://www.landis.org.uk/soilscapes/ (accessed 24 March 2015)

4 http://www.neighbourhood.statistics.gov.uk/ Usual Resident Population by Parish, 2011 Census (accessed 24 March 2015)

5 Ibid

6 http://www.landis.org.uk/soilscapes/ (accessed 24 March 2015)

7 Bowler 1968, 220

8 Defoe 1724–6 (1971 reprint), 131; Hasted 1798, 2

9 Bilbe 2013, 13

10 Gibson 1754, 177

11 Anon 1810, 3D

12 Booker 2007, 30–1; MacDougall 1980, 166; Gurney 1824

13 Anon 2000

14 Moore 2002, 269

15 Miles 1968; Miles 1975

16 Preston 1977

17 Ibid, 54

18 Pateman 2007, 73–5

19 James 2007, 25

20 Hadfield 1969, 94

21 Hazell 2001, 9

22 Hart 1989

23 Cooper-Key 1908

24 Matthews 1995, 103

25 Anon nd, 6

26 Guillery and Williams 1995, unpaginated

27 Smith 1985, 43

28 MacDougall 1980a, 7

29 Smith 2001, 51

30 The National Archives, PRO: WO 192/48

31 Evans 2006, 66

32 Ibid, 92

33 Ibid, 172

34 The National Archives, PRO WO 33/683

35 The National Archives, PRO AIR 1/645/17/122/329

36 Bilbe 2013, 11–12

37 Small 2014, 1

38 MacDougall 1980, 146

39 Edgeworth 2013, 66

40 Carpenter 2014

41 Draper 2010, 69

42 Hazell 2011, 11

43 Greatorex 2005

44 Yates 2007, Fig 3.3; Table 3

45 James 1999

46 Bowler 1968, 9; Witney 1989, 30

47 Bowler 1968, 1

48 Ibid, 2

49 Bannister 2011, 47

50 Draper 2013, 10

51 Edwards and Lake 2012, 13; Campbell 2010, 33

52 Edwards and Lake 2012, 26

53 Mate 2010, 2

54 Edwards and Lake 2012, 153

55 Anon 1903, 189

56 Russell 1695 A plot of Cliffe Level, Kent History and Library Centre S/NK/P/8a; *see* Fig 60

57 Bannister 2011, 47

58 Newman 2012, 249

59 MacDougall 1980, 128–9

60 B Edwards, unpublished notes on Hoo Peninsula Historic Farmstead Characterisation

61 Anon 1914, 1

62 http://www.haven.com/parks/kent/allhallows/ (accessed 24 March 2015)

Project results

Further information and more detailed references can be found in the following reports:

Analytical Aerial Survey Data (source: Historic England Archive and www.pastscape.org.uk)

Bannister, N 2011 *Hoo Peninsula Historic Landscape Project: Historic Landscape Characterisation and Historic Seascape Characterisation Module [EH5733].* Report for English Heritage (source: Historic England Archive or Kent County Council)

Bannister, N 2012 *Hoo Peninsula Historic Landscape Project: Historic Landscape Characterisation and Historic Seascape Characterisation Modules [EH5733] Stage 2. Integrative Analysis.* Report for English Heritage (source: Historic England Archive or Kent County Council)

Carpenter, E 2014 *Halstow Marshes, High Halstow, Hoo Peninsula, Kent: Halstow Marshes Decoy Pond.* English Heritage Research Report 17-2014 (source: http://research.historicengland.org.uk/redirect.aspx?id=6270)

Carpenter, E 2014 *The London Stones: Marking the City of London's Jurisdiction over the Thames and Medway.* English Heritage Research Report 16-2014 (source: http://research.historicengland.org.uk/redirect.aspx?id=6187)

Carpenter, E, Newsome, S, Small, F and Hazell, Z 2013 *Hoo Peninsula, Kent: Hoo Peninsula Historic Landscape Project.* English Heritage Research Report Series 21-2013 (source: http://research.historicengland.org.uk/redirect.aspx?id=6108)

Clarke, J and Smith, J 2014 *Cliffe and Cliffe Woods, Hoo Peninsula, Kent: Historic Area Assessment.* English Heritage Research Report Series 54-2014 (source: http://research.historicengland.org.uk/redirect.aspx?id=6260)

Clarke, J and Smith, J 2014 *Cooling, Hoo Peninsula, Kent: Historic Area Assessment.* English Heritage Research Report Series 51-2014 (source: http://research.historicengland.org.uk/redirect.aspx?id=6256)

Clarke, J and Smith, J 2014 *High Halstow, Hoo Peninsula, Kent: Historic Area Assessment.* English Heritage Research Report Series 53-2014 (source: http://research.historicengland.org.uk/redirect.aspx?id=6257)

Clarke, J and Smith, J 2014 *St Mary Hoo, Hoo Peninsula, Kent: Historic Area Assessment.* English Heritage Research Report Series 52-2014 (source: http://research.historicengland.org.uk/redirect.aspx?id=6155)

Edgeworth, M 2013 *Grain Island Firing Point, Yantlet Creek, Isle of Grain, Medway: Archaeological Desk-based Assessment.* English Heritage Research Report Series 39-2013 (source: http://research.historicengland.org.uk/redirect.aspx?id=6124)

Edwards, B and Lake, J 2012 *Kent Farmsteads and Landscapes Project.* Forum Heritage Services on behalf of English Heritage and Kent County Council (source: Historic England Archive or Kent County Council)

Gregory, D and Newsome, S 2010 *Cooling Radio Station, Hoo Peninsula, Kent: An Archaeological Investigation of a Short-wave Receiving Station.* English Heritage Research Department Report Series 110-2010 (source: http://research.historicengland.org.uk/redirect.aspx?id=5942)

Hazell, Z 2011 *Hoo Peninsula, North Kent Coast, Thames Estuary: A Palaeoenvironmental Review of the Development of the Peninsula.* English Heritage Research Department Report Series 14-2011 (source: http://research.historicengland.org.uk/redirect.aspx?id=5961)

Historic Landscape Characterisation Data (source: Historic England Archive or Kent County Council)

Historic Seascape Characterisation Data (source: Historic England Archive or Kent County Council)

Newsome, S and Pullen, R 2013 *St Mary's Marshes, Hoo St Mary, Medway, Kent: An Assessment of the Late 19th Century Explosives Magazines.* English Heritage Research Report Series 52-2013

(source: http://research.historicengland.org.uk/redirect. aspx?id=6135)

Palaeoenvironmental Review Data (source: Historic England Archive)

Pullen, R, Newsome, S, Williams, A and Cocroft, WD 2011 *Curtis's and Harvey Ltd Explosives Factory, Cliffe and Cliffe Woods, Medway: Archaeological Survey and Analysis of the Factory Remains*. English Heritage Research Department Report Series 11-2011 (source: http://research.historicengland.org.uk/redirect. aspx?i=14963)

Small, F 2014 *Second World War Oil QF Bombing Decoy, Allhallows, Kent*. English Heritage Research Report 8-2014 (source: http://research.historicengland.org.uk/redirect.aspx?id=6180)

Smith, J 2014 *Isle of Grain, Hoo Peninsula, Kent: Historic Area Assessment*. English Heritage Research Report 1-2014 (source: http://research.historicengland.org.uk/redirect.aspx?id=6176)

Smith, J 2014 *The Parish of Allhallows, Hoo Peninsula, Kent: Historic Area Assessment*. English Heritage Research Report Series 11-2014 (source: http://research.historicengland.org.uk/redirect. aspx?id=6182)

Smith, J 2014 *The Parish of Stoke, Hoo Peninsula, Kent: Historic Area Assessment*. English Heritage Research Report Series 12-2014 (source: http://research.historicengland.org.uk/redirect. aspx?id=6183)

Truscoe, K (forthcoming) *Hoo Peninsula, Kent: Second World War Stop Line, Hoo St Werburgh to Higham Marshes*. English Heritage Research Report Series 9-2014 (source: http://research. historicengland.org.uk/)

Williams A and Newsome S (forthcoming) *Cliffe Fort, Hoo Peninsula, Medway, Kent: Investigation and Analysis of the 19th Coastal Artillery Fort*. English Heritage Research Department Report Series 15-2011 (source: http://research.historicengland. org.uk/)

References

Anon nd *A Guide for Visitors to BP's Kent Oil Refinery and Tanker Terminal, Isle of Grain*. BP

Anon 1810 *The Times*. 13 Feb 1810

Anon 11 Jul 1914 *Chatham, Rochester & Gillingham News*

Anon 2000 *European Landscape Convention*. Strasbourg: Council of Europe

Bannister, N 2011 *Hoo Peninsula Historic Landscape Project: Historic Landscape Characterisation and Historic Seascape Characterisation Module [EH5733]*. Report for English Heritage

Bilbe, T 2013 *Kingsnorth Airship Station: In Defence of the Nation*. Stroud: The History Press

Booker, J 2007 *Maritime Quarantine: The British Experience c.1650–1900*. Farnham: Ashgate

Bowler, E 1968 *The Reclamation and Land Use of the Thames Marshes of North West Kent*. Unpublished PhD dissertation, Geography Dept., LSE

Campbell, BMS 2010 'Agriculture in Kent in the High Middle Ages' *in* Sweetinburgh, S (ed) *Later Medieval Kent 1220–1540*. Woodbridge: The Boydell Press and Kent County Council

Carpenter, E 2014 *The London Stones: Marking the City of London's Jurisdiction over the Thames and Medway*. English Heritage Research Report 16-2014

Cooper-Key, A 1908 *No CLXXXIV Report to the Right Honourable the Secretary of State for the Home Department on the Circumstances attending an Explosion which occurred in a Cartridge Hut at the Factory of Messrs Curtis's and Harvey Limited at Cliffe in the county of Kent, on the 5th June 1908*. London: HMSO

Defoe, D 1724–6 *A Tour Through the Whole Island of Great Britain*. (1971 repr) London: Penguin

Draper, G 2010 'Timber and iron: Natural resources for the Late Medieval shipbuilding industry in Kent (c.1350–1500)' *in* Sweetinburgh, S (ed) *Later Medieval Kent 1220–1540*. Woodbridge: The Boydell Press and Kent County Council

Draper, G 2013 *Hoo Marshland Field Systems 6384*. Unpublished Report for English Heritage

Edgeworth, M 2013 *Grain Island Firing Point, Yantlet Creek, Isle of Grain, Medway: Archaeological Desk-based Assessment*. English Heritage Research Report 39-2013

Edwards, B and Lake, J 2012 *Kent Farmsteads and Landscape Project*. Report for English Heritage and Kent County Council

Evans, D 2006 *Arming the Fleet: The Development of the Royal Ordnance Yards 1770–1945*. Explosion Museum with English Heritage

Gelling, M and Cole, A 2003 *The Landscape of Place-names*. Stamford: Shaun Tyas

Gibson, W 1754 *A New Treatise on the Disease of Horses*. London: A Millar

Greatorex, C 2005 'Later Prehistoric settlement on the Hoo Peninsula: Excavations at Kingsmead Park, Allhallows'. *Archaeologia Cantiana* **125**, 67–81

Guillery, P and Williams, M 1995 *The Power Stations of the Lower Thames*. Swindon: RCHME

Gurney, WB 1824 *Yantlet Creek: Rex versus James Montague, William Lambert Newman, John Nelson and four others: report of the trial on an indictment against the defendants*. Available online at https://books.google.co.uk/books?id=CrEHAAAAQAAJ&printsec=frontcover&source=gbs_ge_summary_#v=onepage&q&f=false

Hadfield, C 1969 *The Canals of South and South East England*. Newton Abbot: David and Charles

Hart, B 1989 *The Hundred of Hoo Railway*. Didcot: Wild Swan Publications

Hasted, E 1798 *The History and Topographical Survey of the County of Kent* **4**. Canterbury: W Bristow

Hazell, M 2001 *Sailing Barges*. Princess Risborough: Shire

Hazell, Z 2011 *Hoo Peninsula, North Kent Coast, Thames Estuary: A Palaeoenvironmental Review of the Development of the Peninsula*. English Heritage Research Department Report Series 14-2011

James, R 1999 *Archaeological Excavations at Middle Stoke*, 1995 and 1998. Project Number 853. Portslade: Archaeology South-East

James, R 2007 *Historic Environment Desk-based Assessment Cliffe Pools RSPB Reserve Kent*. Portslade: Archaeology South-East

Kelly & Co 1903 *Kelly's Directory of Kent*. London: Kelly & Co

Lake, J, Edwards, B and Banister, N 2014 'Farmsteads and landscapes in Kent', *Archaeologia Cantiana* **134**, 105–39

MacDougall, P 1980 *The Story of the Hoo Peninsula*. Rochester: John Hallewell

MacDougall, P 1980a *The Isle of Grain Defences*. Northfleet: Kent Defence Research Group

Mate, M 2010 'The Economy of Kent 1200–1500: An Age of Expansion, 1200–1348' *in* Sweetinburgh, S (ed) *Later Medieval Kent 1220–1540*. Woodbridge: The Boydell Press and Kent County Council

Matthews, P 1995 *Guinness Book of Records*. London: Guinness World Records Ltd

Miles, A 1968 'Romano-British salt panning hearths at Cliffe'. *Archaeologia Cantiana*, **88**, 272–3

Miles, A 1975 'Salt-panning in Romano-British Kent' *in* de Brisay, KW & Evans, KA (eds) *Salt: The Study of an Ancient Industry*. Colchester: Colchester Archaeological Group

Mills, AD 2003 *A Dictionary of British Place Names*. Oxford: Oxford University Press

Moore, C 2002 'Late Bronze Age, Romano-British and Early/Middle Saxon features at Hoo St. Werburgh' *Archaeologia Cantiana*, **122**, 259–74

Newman, J 2012 *The Buildings of England: Kent: West and the Weald*. New Haven and London: Yale University Press

Pateman, J 2007 *Hoo, Hops and Hods: The Life and Times of Robert Pateman*. Lincolnshire: Pateran Press

Preston, J 1977 *Industrial Medway: An Historical Survey*. Rochester: Preston

Small, F 2014 *Allhallows, Medway, Kent: Second World War Oil QF Bombing Decoy*. English Heritage Research Report 8-2014

Smith, V 1985 *Defending London's River*. Rochester: North Kent Books

Smith, V 2001 *Front-Line Kent Defence against Invasion from 1400 to the Cold War*. Maidstone: Kent County Council

Witney, KP 1989 'Development of the Kentish marshes in the aftermath of the Norman Conquest'. *Archaeologia Cantiana* **107**, 29–50

Yates, D 2007 *Land, Power and Prestige: Bronze Age Field Systems in Southern England*. Oxford: Oxbow

Informed Conservation Series

This popular Historic England series highlights the special character of some of our most important historic areas and the development pressures they are facing. There are over 30 titles in the series, some of which look at whole towns such as Bridport, Coventry and Margate or distinctive urban districts, such as the Jewellery Quarter in Birmingham and Ancoats in Manchester, while others focus on particular building types in a particular place. A few are national in scope focusing, for example, on English school buildings and garden cities.

The purpose of the series is to raise awareness in a non-specialist audience of the interest and importance of aspects of the built heritage of towns and cities undergoing rapid change or large-scale regeneration. A particular feature of each book is a final chapter that focuses on conservation issues, identifying good examples of the re-use of historic buildings and highlighting those assets or areas for which significant challenges remain.

As accessible distillations of more in-depth research, they also provide a useful resource for heritage professionals, tackling, as many of the books do, places and buildings types that have not previously been subjected to investigation from the historic environment perspective. As well as providing a lively and informed discussion of each subject, the books also act as advocacy documents for Historic England and its partners in promoting the management of change in the historic environment.

More information on each of the books in the series and on forthcoming titles, together with links to enable them to be ordered or downloaded is available on the Historic England website.

HistoricEngland.org.uk